DISCIPLE MAKING
AMONG HINDUS

DISCIPLE MAKING AMONG HINDUS

मार्ग

MAKING AUTHENTIC RELATIONSHIPS GROW

TIMOTHY SHULTZ

WILLIAM CAREY
LIBRARY

Published by William Carey Library, an imprint of William Carey Publishing
10 W. Dry Creek Circle
Littleton, CO 80120 | www.missionbooks.org

Aidan Lewis, editor
Sharon Edwards, copyeditor
Josie Leung, graphic design

William Carey Library is a ministry of Frontier Ventures
Pasadena, CA 91104 | www.frontierventures.org

23 22 21 20 19 Printed for Worldwide Distribution

Library of Congress Cataloging-in-Publication Data
Names: Shultz, Timothy, author.
Title: Disciple making among Hindus : making authentic relationships grow /
    Timothy Shultz.
Description: Pasadena, CA : William Carey Library, 2016. | Includes
    bibliographical references.
Identifiers: LCCN 2016032557 (print) | LCCN 2016033010 (ebook) |
    ISBN13: 9780878081387 (pbk.) | ISBN10: 0878081380 (pbk.) | ISBN
    9780878086818 (eBook)
Subjects: LCSH: Christianity and other religions--Hinduism. |
    Hinduism--Relations--Christianity. | Missions to Hindus. | Discipling
    (Christianity)
Classification: LCC BR128.H5 S545 2016 (print) | LCC BR128.H5 (ebook) |
    DDC
    261.2/45--dc23
LC record available at https://lccn.loc.gov/2016032557

To my wonderful wife, Melanie:
You are the only reason why, apart from God.
Asante sana mara vahalla.
All my love.

CONTENTS

मार्ग

INTRODUCTION

IT WAS A beautiful August evening. The air was delightfully warm and pleasant, making the sheer white curtain at the window flutter lightly. My young children sat on the floor of the enclosed porch playing with their toys, their innocent laughter carried to our ears on the summer breeze.

I was sitting on the couch with my friend Ashok, a man of about thirty who had recently migrated to the United States from Kolkata (formerly Calcutta), capital of the Indian state of West Bengal. We chatted about this and that, feeling no need to engage in a serious conversation. As our conversation turned to his life in India, Ashok became quiet and his eyes held a distant expression. I could tell that he was reliving something from the past, so I waited, giving him space to ponder and process the memory that had risen.

He finally turned toward me and said in a quiet but firm voice, "You and Bhabiji do not really understand what it was like for me before I began praying to Lord Jesus. I had lived for years in fear of the many gods and goddesses of my people, but I am no longer afraid. Believe me, brother, I would not have known the truth if I had not come here to America. That is why God brought me here."

Ashok refers to my wife as "Bhabiji," a respectful way of addressing a sister-in-law in Hindi. He went on to tell me that he was planning a trip to India to see his father, who was critically ill and might die. He also wanted to visit a friend who was an influential person in a Hindu temple and share his testimony with that man. We talked about the trip and then prayed that God would fulfill His plans.

While in India, it became apparent that his father would indeed not survive. Ashok told him about his devotion to Jesus, and was relieved and overjoyed when his father blessed him in his new faith. His friend in the temple had never heard the gospel before, and Ashok shared with him at length, although his friend was not really open to that. When he returned to the US, we had a memorial for his father. The ceremony looked very Hindu externally, but it was completely Christ-centered at the core. It remains one of the high points of my life.

Ashok is from a higher caste Hindu family. He came to the US to cash in on the American dream, but instead he found true riches in Jesus Christ. Ashok is among the millions of Hindus who are migrating all over the world, including to the US. This huge population shift, which has no end in sight, is clearly an act of God to bring the gospel to people. As the apostle Paul says in his famous sermon on Mars Hill,

> The God who made the world and everything in it is the Lord of heaven and earth and does not live in temples built by hands. And he is not served by human hands, as if he needed anything, because he gives all men life and breath and everything else. From one man he made every nation of men that they should inhabit the whole earth, and he determined the times set for them and the exact places where they should live. God did this so that men would seek him and perhaps reach out for him and find him, though he is not far from each of us. (Acts 17:24–27)

This dense and life-altering passage of Scripture is saying that God actively determines the movements and destinies of the peoples of the earth, even to the extent of arranging where they live, so they will find Jesus. It confirms that the millions of Hindus moving all over the world are being moved by God, so that they can be saved. *God* arranged for this.

In the vast majority of examples, people are saved as they encounter a believer who shares the gospel with them, helping them to believe. As Ashok so astutely pointed out to me, that is why God has brought him here.

The world is vastly different from what it once was. It is not 1880 on a mission compound in the Punjab, or even 1980 at a Christian college in South India anymore. The missionary era of legend and lore in India is long over. Many people think that is actually a good thing. I am one of those who do—even though in moments of tedious, unfulfilling work, I wonder what it would have been like to be a missionary in Bangalore or Lahore in 1920.

Despite dramatic changes in the world and in India, disciple-making ministry hasn't changed that much in the early decades of the twenty-first century. Global ministry is still often understood to be usually Western Christian missionaries going somewhere to convert non-Christians. In this philosophy of ministry, the world is conceived of in terms of the Christian and the non-Christian areas of the world. Europe, North America (excluding Mexico), and Australia are considered Christian, and most other places are not—or not *quite*—Christian. Many from Protestant denominations think Latin America is not really Christian because of the predominance of Catholicism. To put it simply, the Christian world sends missionaries to the non-Christian world to establish or grow the apostolic faith there.

Discipleship that has implemented this philosophy usually appears in the form of missionaries building a Christian infrastructure within the non-Christian world, causing Christianity to spread globally. Historically, this approach has been remarkably successful in many parts of the world, and I enjoy reading stories of missionaries who served in this manner in sub-Saharan Africa, parts of Asia, and Latin America. Many of those missionaries are my heroes. However, the paradigm no longer represents a realistic view of what God is doing in the world. Christendom no longer exists as a meaningful religious or even cultural construct, and many of the nations outside of the old husk of Christendom are now much more "Christian" than Europe and her Protestant or Catholic offspring in North America and Australia.

The new world is not neatly divided between Christian and non-Christian. The global diaspora of peoples from nearly everywhere to just about anywhere must do nothing less than revolutionize how we conceive of Christianity and mission. Without a doubt, the incredible globalization that largely defines the twenty-first century is marked by the fingerprints of God. God is arranging the economies of the world to become more "globalized" than ever—but not so a few can get even richer than they already are or so a few more can get good IT jobs. God is creating a platform to connect people who have greater access to the gospel with those who have less.

It's about people, not places.

In this new world, awareness of the need to focus disciple making toward higher caste Hindus is growing. God is working in unprecedented ways to bring these people the opportunity to hear the gospel, often for the first time. The global movement of millions of Hindus from South Asia, and the connections that are being forged between this global diaspora and their family and friends who remain in South Asia, is part of a significant contemporary movement of God to extend greater opportunity for Hindus to hear the gospel.

Those who are sent to Hindus within South Asia and those who receive the global Hindu diaspora are both equally a part of God's work. Both are vital, and networking between these two modes of mission can be synergistically and exponentially explosive to the growth of the gospel. I am always encouraged when I hear that Christians are sharing the gospel with Hindu people no matter who they are or where they live. Yet what thrills me most is the unspoken message I "hear" when people want to discuss the issues surrounding communicating the gospel to Hindus. More and more mission-minded people seem to know that we must bring Jesus to people as well as bring *people* to *Jesus*. In other words, we must live within the world in such a way that our life in Christ is accessible to people who do not yet believe the gospel, so they can see Jesus living in us and through us. Jesus himself is the pattern for this, for he lived among people as the very Son of God, bringing the rule and reign of God into their lives. In this incarnational way of life, we bring Jesus to people. We also bring people to Jesus. We must be able to verbalize the good news of the death, resurrection, and lordship of Jesus Christ, and the opportunity that everyone has to become his disciple, receiving salvation from sin and death and membership in the kingdom of God through faith in Jesus.

I also find that many Christians today are deeply committed to a value system that includes respect for people from other cultures and religious backgrounds, even as they passionately follow Jesus within their own way of life. This is spiritually healthy and brings glory to God by recognizing the global nature of his kingdom. These Christians also deeply desire to bring Jesus to a person in ways that speak to his or her heart, so that Jesus is exalted at the deepest level of that person's life. This is vastly different from the earlier mode of advocating that Hindus adopt a certain style of Christianity.

Based on my observations, people truly want to be fruitful in their ministry to Hindus. They want to know that they have done the best they possibly could to translate the gospel to their Hindu friends in word and deed, through the living testimony of their way of life as well as by communicating the gospel. They feel this way because they are in relationship with Hindus and feel personally invested in the lives of Hindu families. I am also greatly encouraged that these types of encounters almost never involve counting numbers of converts in a retail manner of ministry.

The reader will note the subtitle of this book, *Making Authentic Relationships Grow*. The first letter of each word spells the acronym MARG. *Marg*, or *marga*, is a Sanskrit word used in just about any Hindu religiocultural context to mean "path" or "journey." While it has a generic literal usage, it is almost always used to mean a religious or spiritual path that one walks over time toward *moksha*, or the Hindu concept of salvation. Understanding the significance of *marg* and how it is related to discipleship of Hindu people is critical to the philosophy of discipleship presented in this book. I have learned over many years that just as Hindus journey gradually toward moksha, so also they travel toward discipleship to Jesus.

I previously published a small booklet called "MARG: Making Authentic Relationships Grow," which was so well received that I decided to develop it further into the present book. Here I have presented the MARG, or path, of discipleship to Jesus. My earnest desire is that it will help you love and disciple Hindu people and their families. This book is not theoretical, nor is it a strategy of contextualization that I came up with in an office filled with books and whiteboards. It is more than an attempt to explain how we can be more successful in evangelistic outreach. *Disciple Making among Hindus* is a testimony of the kingdom growing in a non-Christian environment and an attempt to explain the patterns of what I and others have been doing as Hindu people have responded to Jesus.

As you read this book, you may come across points of view that you find challenging. Perhaps they seem counterintuitive or even dangerous. I can fully identify with that, because everything I have written here I continue to experience as a journey of discovery that stretches me. I was raised as a Christian—a very conservative one, at that—and I was exposed to some teaching that was, frankly, quite narrow-minded and needlessly separatist: a sort of "We love God, but we don't like you very much" approach to Christian life. As a result, I have been wrestling and trying to understand the depth and breadth of the kingdom of God for a number of years.

To be honest, on more than one occasion I have sincerely wondered if I had gone too far and unintentionally compromised the truth. In fact, I probably *did* cross the syncretism line at times, but I found that God's grace abounded there as I identified with people who were trying to find their way to Jesus outside of any Christian heritage or culture. I did not intentionally choose compromise, which would have been foolish and presumptuous. I only willingly chose an incarnational life for Jesus with Hindu families.

That choice sent me out of accepted local church–centered Christian practice and witness into the non-Christian world, where the only clear things were the lordship of Jesus and the authority of the Bible. And I found that Jesus was already there. In fact, he had drawn me there to reveal himself to me more fully. He is so gracious.

मार्ग

CHAPTER 1

LEARNING CURVE

WE WILL BEGIN by looking at some ways of understanding the gospel in terms that are already meaningful to Hindus. Instead of giving them a new language, we use the spiritual terms with which they are already familiar. These terms function as a bridge.

MERCY AND POWER

Whenever we dare—and dare we must—to consider personally addressing the need of humankind to hear and believe the gospel, we must always begin and end our soul-searching with a humble recognition of the benevolent power and incomparable mercy of God. In Sanskrit terms, we should practice this *sadhana* (spiritual discipline) of contemplation intentionally and carefully, because a wholesome understanding of how God acts in powerful mercy and merciful power does not come easily or naturally to us. Instead, we tend to automatically assume that God acts according to the pattern of the world in which we live. In this world, powerful people often exercise their authority with an agenda that corrupts any semblance of mercy. Living in an environment that functions this way can distort our vision of God's merciful power and powerful mercy. God's power and mercy are an extension of his goodness, so he does not act like powerful people in the world.

God's *karuna* (mercy) and *shakti* (power) were put on display when his Son, the Lord Jesus Christ, *Guruji Muktidatta Abhishikta* (the Savior and Anointed One), took *samadhi* (choosing to leave the body) on a cruel Roman cross. Three days later, Jesus returned to life in the same perfected body because his *atma* (spirit) was pure and did not take another form. Now, he is the Lord of *karma*, and he is merciful. His mercy is incomparable precisely because he is so powerful. Because he is mercifully powerful, he doesn't give us what we deserve—and because he is powerfully merciful, he gives us what we don't. This reveals a lot about the nature of God and draws us to trust him.

God is also very generous by nature, so he frequently exerts his power in order to show mercy to vast numbers of people all over the world. This means that we must base any recognition of and response to the need for humankind to hear the gospel on the fact that God is perfectly willing to finally and fully bring justice and mercy to bear in human affairs. *We* serve the mission of *God*, not the other way around.

Often, when the gospel message is clearly and appropriately articulated to Hindus, it comes as the consummation or explanation of the *experience* of that unprecedented power and mercy. All this while they may have wondered, "Why is God providing for us or healing us or delivering us when we approach him in Jesus' name?" Or, "Why am I drawn to approach Jesus, which is the last thing I ever thought I would do?" When the gospel is presented to them in terms they understand, they realize that Jesus himself is the good news, and his story is the message of God's power and mercy.

HINDU SOCIETY AND HINDU COMMUNITY

The global Hindu population comprises over one billion people. Despite this large number, there is no one "Hindu nation" (although

Nepal was officially a Hindu state until 2007). There have been or are Christian or Muslim nations, but there is no country in the world where everybody is Hindu. Even India, which is largely Hindu, is nowhere near to being a Hindu country; before too long it will claim some 200 million Muslims and between 35 and 50 million Christians, not to mention 25 million Sikhs and significant numbers of Buddhists, Jains, and other religious minorities. Therefore, we need to adjust our view if we are to undertake any sort of analysis of the global Hindu population.

One way we can do this is by categorizing these large numbers of people as Hindu *society* and Hindu *community*. For our purposes here, we will define a Hindu society as a more permanent structure, and a Hindu community as something more temporary or transient.

By far the world's largest Hindu societies are in that ancient and romantic part of the world now referred to as South Asia. India, which has always been the civilizational center of South Asia, is in fact the birthplace of Hindu civilization. It is outside the scope of this book to study the beginnings of Hinduism, but if we were to consider the history of only the twentieth century, we would see how Hinduism exists in the entire region.

At the dawn of the twentieth century, most of the Indian Subcontinent was part of the British Empire. When the British Raj ended in 1947, the Partition of India resulted in the formation of a new country—split into two territories, one to the east and one to the west— called Pakistan. Accordingly, although the modern-day nation of Pakistan is overwhelmingly Muslim, it also has pockets of Hindu societies. East and West Pakistan were divided by the civil war of 1971, out of which was forged the nation of Bangladesh, and there are permanent Bengali Hindu societies in Bangladesh as well. Nepal is majority Hindu, and Sri Lanka has a longstanding Tamil Hindu society. Bhutan, the small landlocked country between India and China, also has a significant percentage of Hindus. Thus, all of these South Asian nations have been a part of the evolution of global Hindu society due to their proximity to India.

Over time, millions of Hindu people have created their own permanent societies in the most unexpected places across the globe, including the Caribbean Islands; Suriname and Guyana on the northern coast of South America; Singapore and Malaysia; Indonesia and Fiji; the UK and the Netherlands; and Mauritius, East Africa, and South Africa. There will soon be three million Hindus living in the US and Canada alone. More recently, permanent Hindu societies are being formed in Australia and New Zealand as well. The technological revolution has guaranteed a steady flow of Indian IT workers to the West, and there is no end in sight to this unprecedented movement of people.

These global Hindu societies tend to drift from a living relationship with "Mother India," but there is still a respect and nostalgic memory of their Indian roots. Ease of travel to and within modern India has now made it possible for Hindu people from global Hindu societies to spend time there, often for the first time.

In addition to Hindu societies, Hindu *communities* also exist in other parts of the world. These are contexts in which the Hindu population is relatively new and has not had the time to settle down, or where the local political situation does not allow a Hindu *society* to form. A Hindu community usually retains living connections to India because they are not yet established in a Hindu society outside of India.

Two examples can be readily cited. In the European Union, a Hindu community is now beginning to form. No doubt as the people settle in various EU countries they will create Hindu societies, but they are still a relatively new population in the region. In contrast, hundreds of thousands of Hindu people have been working in the Middle East for decades and living within their own communities, but the nature of life in the Gulf does not permit them to form a permanent Hindu society. As the world continues to shrink, Hindu societies and communities will undoubtedly proliferate into every corner of the globe, wherever opportunity presents itself.

In many contexts outside of India, Hindu society and community exist together. This happens because there is a longstanding pattern of migration from India into a society of Hindus that has already been established in another country. The process happens something like this: When people and families first leave South Asia and settle in a Hindu society somewhere in the world, such as in the UK or Australia, they remain culturally and emotionally connected to India. They have not yet fused the world of their birthplace with the local world in which they now live. If many of these people migrate at the same time, Hindu communities that are still connected to South Asia will quickly form within the local Hindu society, which is already fused into the new culture. Gradually, these communities of India-centric people become part of the local Hindu society. They will update the existing Hindu culture according to more current trends in South Asia for people who have never lived there and whose Hindu culture may seem a bit dated. They will also themselves integrate into the fusion culture that has emerged locally, updating their own views to fit in. However, no matter how acculturated they might become, the majority of these new immigrants remain *Hindu* at their core.

OPPORTUNITY

I once saw a commercial for a telecom company. The advertising was obviously targeted to grow market share within the globalized Indian community because the commercial showed an Indian woman in New York talking to family members in London and Mumbai on the same day for inexpensive rates. I smiled, knowing that the business world seems to understand what we Christians struggle to see: *opportunity*.

India is and will always be the center of Hindu society and community. What is changing is that the rest of the world is entering into a new era of relationship with India. This global relationship is largely based on the rise of India as a modern economic and democratic power. There have been periods in history when the world spoke in jealous wonder about the power and wealth of ancient India, but India has never been a major player on the global stage as it is today. This means that the people of India are freer to engage the people of the world than they have ever been. As India engages the world and the world engages India, there are unprecedented opportunities to meet the needs of millions of higher caste Hindus who have not yet heard the gospel.

Furthermore, these opportunities for witnessing are not just localized. They are potentially *glocalized*. *Glocal* is a word that combines *local* and *global*. It means that anything that is local also has a global element. The concept does not mean that identical things are local in more than one country. It means that one thing has an essence that enables it to assimilate whatever it encounters all over the world without losing its essence. The global Hindu diaspora is a glocal community. The kingdom of God is also glocal.

When believers in Christ who live in Chicago, London, New Delhi, or Singapore invest their lives in relationships with their Hindu neighbors locally, they can literally see that witness spread globally, because in the glocal higher caste Hindu community of the twenty-first century, bringing the gospel to Hindus anywhere is potentially bringing the gospel to them *everywhere*. Those who are sent within South Asia and those who are sent within the Hindu diaspora are both parts of God's working in the world. Both are vital, and networking between these two modes of mission can be synergistically and exponentially explosive to the spread of the gospel.

Caste and culture deeply affect this call to share the gospel with Hindu people. Historically, the lower castes have been more responsive to the gospel, so they have naturally received the majority of the ministry. Conversely, the higher castes and upper socioeconomic classes have not been nearly as responsive, and so they have received very little ministry. And this is true not only in India but elsewhere in the world as well.

This raises a question that we must all take at least a moment to ponder. Do higher caste Hindu people fail to respond to the gospel and therefore receive little or no ministry, or do higher caste Hindu people receive very little ministry and therefore fail to respond? Regardless of how one answers this question, higher caste Hindus are at the epicenter of the least reached peoples of the earth, and they may number as many as *400 million.* That's a truly staggering figure.

WHAT IS HINDUISM?

Most people assume that Hinduism is the ancient religion of the indigenous people of South Asia, specifically of India. Since there are one billion Hindus in the world, Hinduism is often classified as a major world religion. In fact, it is usually listed in textbooks as the third largest religion in the world in terms of adherents, after Christianity and Islam. Most Christian ministry leaders also assume this religious interpretation of Hinduism and conduct gospel ministry on that basis.

The question *What is Hinduism?* is a significant one to consider. If Hinduism is indeed a religion, those who wish to faithfully share the gospel usually insist on conversion away from Hinduism and the need to embrace Christianity. From this perspective, anything less is almost certainly compromise and syncretism. However, if Hinduism is not essentially a religion, then faithful disciple-making ministry must adapt to the reality of translating discipleship to Jesus into Hindu forms and functions.

Obviously, it is vital to make sure that we correctly understand the nature of Hinduism so we will know how to position ourselves toward Hindus as ambassadors of Christ and his kingdom. Since Hinduism is ancient, we need to understand it historically. Since there are one billion Hindus in the world, we also need to understand Hinduism as it is experienced in the lives of contemporary Hindus. This approach will reveal that Hinduism is actually a comprehensive way of life within which the gospel may be translated, rather than a religion that people need to reject in order to confess Christ.

In very general terms, what is now referred to as Hinduism evolved over time in pre-Islamic South Asia. This area would include the contemporary nation of India as well as Pakistan, Bangladesh, Nepal, and Sri Lanka. There was no such thing as "Hinduism" during these long, largely hidden years. Centuries of interaction between the older, more established non-Aryan civilization of ancient South Asia and waves of immigrating and quickly settling Aryan tribes eventually created a highly diverse and complex society that included both religion and culture. The way of life that ultimately became the most dominant was based on the Vedas, the Aryan scriptures. Hindus today revere the Vedas as their foundational scriptures.

Everything that has defined the historical development of any place or people on earth also took place in this region. Empires rose and fell. Diverse expressions of the arts and sciences, of economics and ethics, and of morality and religion all evolved among the many peoples of this subcontinent. Eventually, an unmistakable unity within the diversity developed because various political and cultural movements created civilizational frameworks that brought localized cultures into a larger South Asian world. Everything was part of one civilizational whole that developed over many centuries.

Thus, the key concept that unlocks this "Hindu history" is *integration*, a process that is sometimes referred to as Sanskritization. It is this civilizational ethos that creates the unity within all of the religious and cultural diversity within Hinduism, making it look like one thing—but that one thing is *civilizational*, not *religious*. It was eventually called Hinduism, first by the Islamic and then by the British overlords of South Asia, or India.

The word *Hindu* itself was originally used to identify the geographic area east of the Indus River. The Islamic invaders, traders, and missionaries who came from the west had to ford it to reach the fabled land of jewels and spices that ultimately became known as *Hindustan*.

Over time, *Hindu* also began to refer to the *people* who lived in this region east of the Indus. The religious connotations emerged afterwards, when the Islamic rulers and those of Christendom began to interact with the indigenous peoples and understand their religious beliefs and practices.

Hindus see the civilizational period of South Asian history prior to the influence of the Islamic and Christian colonial powers as their golden age, and they draw their identity from it. However, there is currently a dangerous and dark side to this interpretation of Hinduism. It is not only tinged with understandable anger over colonial abuse and oppression, but it has also become a locus of coercive political power.

Highly influential and politically powerful forces of Hindu nationalism in India are now seeking to make *India* and *Hindu* synonymous terms. In other words, they claim that everything truly Indian is Hindu. This philosophy has led to persecution—sometimes very violent persecution—of Muslims and Christians, who are condemned as non-Indians for having converted to the religion of the foreign oppressors of India or, in their thinking, of *Hinduism*. Many Hindus strongly oppose this approach to Hindu civilization, but an alarming number do not.

Ancient South Asian civilization, or Hinduism, exists today within one of the most socially and culturally diverse and complex countries in the world. India is 80 percent Hindu, but it also has the world's second largest Muslim population and is home to ten million Buddhists! Apart from Buddhism, India is also the birthplace of Jainism and Sikhism, and it has a large and growing Christian population. The Hindu civilization is also global; it has burst its South Asian boundaries, and many thousands of Hindus are now pouring out of India every year.

What this means is that it is no longer really possible to reassert Hinduism as the civilization of India. India is now a leading player on the world stage. It is a liberal democracy with a thriving, modernizing economy and nuclear capability. If Hinduism as civilization is politicized, India loses. If Hinduism is connected to values, India wins. For this to happen, Hinduism must be seen from its historical perspective, as *more than a religion*.

In order for us to be truly relevant as we bring the gospel in our time, we must also consider the beliefs and practices of contemporary Hinduism, especially in relationship with Hindu people. While there are obvious religious elements, such as the well-developed theologies that exist within the various sects of Hinduism, there are also elements that are usually conceived of as *culture*, such as the many unique relationship structures within the families of Hindu people, or the customs of millions of rural Hindu people in villages.

Interaction with Hindu people further reveals that in addition to discrete categories of religion and culture within a Hindu family, community, or society, there are also significant areas in which religion and culture meld into a single way of life, some of it dating back over a thousand years into the early history of South Asia. One clear example of this is an ornate, colorful, chaotic Hindu wedding: we can refer to that as neither exclusively religious nor exclusively cultural, but *religiocultural*. This blended way of life is Hinduism.

It is critical to have a working definition of religion and culture that empowers our understanding of a particular Hindu society or community. This is an obvious first step on the journey toward developing fruitful gospel witness. Westerners should not assume that Hindus fully share their religious and cultural concepts and definitions, as most of these developed in Christian Europe, the Islamic Middle East, and ancient Judaism. In fact, when the words *religion* and *culture* are used to describe specific words and categories from Hinduism, they can lead to confusion and even error. Insisting that this Hindi word is religious, and that Telugu word is cultural, for example, can lead to an incomplete or incorrect understanding of those terms.

This does not mean, however, that it is impossible to use English as a medium to explain the nature of Hinduism. It is important to remember that India is now an English-speaking country. It simply means that we have to be precise about the meaning of words. Precision produces clarity and clarity leads to simplicity, so we have tried to precisely define religion and culture as they relate to the nature of Hinduism.

We are also seeking to define religion and culture with a view to gospel witness. This approach allows room for Hindus to give those who live on mission within Hindu societies or communities anywhere in the world the necessary details of how the words *religion* and *culture* are used locally, a key aspect of effective cross-cultural ministry.

So let us attempt simple but precise definitions of these two terms. By *religion* we mean how the closed groups of Hindu people who live within a Hindu society or community conceive of and relate to God. By *culture* we mean the shared knowledge and customs, including religious faith and practice, that bind together the closed groups of Hindu people who live within a Hindu society or community.

Based on these definitions, Hinduism—as it is interpreted from the long history of South Asia and experienced in the lives of contemporary Hindu people—is a unique synergy of religion and culture that is greater than the sum of its parts. We ultimately learn to conceive of Hinduism as *the way of life that Hindus most value.* Perhaps the most clear and reliable understanding we can have of Hinduism as we go forward into the twenty-first century is that it is a comprehensive and organic unity of values. These values, which are the essence of Hinduism as the Hindu people experience it, are referred to as *dharma.*

In his book *Understanding Hinduism*, Dayanand Bharati defines Hinduism as dharma and dharma as values. He writes, "The most basic point to grasp is that Hinduism is not a religion like other religions but a dharma. . . . So for an average person, dharma is a comprehensive word which includes spiritual, moral, social and even secular values" (2005, 21).

Religion and culture as distinct elements of Hinduism, and the points where Hindu culture and religion fuse, all fall within the rubric of dharma—the values upon which Hindu people build their way of life. In fact, many Hindus use *Sanatan Dharma*, or "eternal dharma," instead of Hinduism to identify their religion and culture.

Hinduism, then, is an organic and living reality, an ancient civilization, a religious aspiration and cultural tradition, joining and separating within the collective memory of the Hindu people as they create and re-create a contemporary way of life based on their values in their societies and communities.

Believers in Christ who seek to effectively share the gospel with Hindu people should concentrate their learning efforts on understanding the particular dharmic values of the local Hindu society and/or community in which they live, because those values are touchpoints for the gospel to address and clarify. Operating from Bharati's definition of Hinduism as dharma and dharma as values also allows Hindus who are open to considering the lordship of Christ to objectively and graciously interpret what they see in their lives and the lives of other Hindus under the light of the gospel, thus empowering discipleship and possible movements of Hindu people to Christ.

There are three ways by which Hindus may respond positively to what the Spirit of God tells them about their dharma. These ways are not unique to Hindus: Christians, Muslims, and indeed *every* group of people across the globe experience the gospel in the same manner.

- First, the gospel may *reveal* the glory of God found within certain values of Hindu dharma, surprising the people with the revelation that Jesus is, at least to that specific extent, a lot like them.
- Second, the gospel may *clarify* the need to believe what Christ has said about his kingdom values that is incompatible with Hindu dharma.
- Third, the gospel may also *redeem* certain Hindu values through the full biblical revelation of the gospel of Jesus Christ, removing that which does not glorify God and then returning that to the Hindu people for their fullest enjoyment as well as for God's glory.

One cannot overstate the importance of demonstrating love, patience, and humility as we reach Hindus with the gospel. It is equally important for us to trust that they are responding to the Spirit, even when it does not look like anything is happening. As Christ's disciples we must be extremely careful not to be too prescriptive in how we come alongside Hindu people as they assess how the gospel changes their dharma—as it most certainly will do. The gospel changes everything and everyone because Jesus is Lord, and we can trust that he will bring forth his kingdom within Hindu societies and communities.

Since Hindus view Christianity as a dharma as well, they rightly assume that the way of life that Christians follow is based on their values. Therefore, disciples of Christ must integrate the values of Jesus into their lives individually and corporately, as the body of Christ. They must also be able to share the values of Jesus with Hindus as a basis upon which to lead them to faith in Christ.

THE HINDU FAMILY

Family is the most important aspect of the life of Hindu people. The vision of the loving, wise, prosperous, resilient, and triumphant traditional Hindu family is the most powerful icon within Hindu culture. It is also becoming increasingly unattainable, but the more that modernity threatens this ideal, the stronger and more intoxicating it seems to become. The longing for such a family is clearly portrayed in many Bollywood films.

The traditional Hindu family is an extended family that resembles the Western idea of a clan. It includes grandparents, parents, children, uncles, aunts, and cousins of closer or further relationship. As a patrilineal culture, it traces its lineage through the men of the family. The grandfathers will naturally stay in very close touch with their brothers and their brothers' families. They may even all stay together in the same large house or housing development (called a housing society in India). When traditional Hindu people talk about their family, they usually mean this large group of relatives.

The traditional family stays together and moves forward through the marriage of their sons. Daughters join their husband's family after marriage. Sons are usually expected to stay in the family home after marrying the girl, whom their parents have chosen for them from another family in the same *jati* (caste or community). These arranged marriages take place with various degrees of involvement on the part of the bride and groom, depending on the family; but all traditional Hindu families prefer heavier parental and familial influence concerning who enters their family through marriage. This is because the next generation is responsible to care for the parents and increase the prosperity that the father or grandfather built. When the families involved are honorable and care about what is best for their children, this method can work quite well.

Traditional Hindus live for the prosperity and security of the family as a whole rather than seeing the family as existing to empower individual success, as is the case in the West. In the better situations, the elders within the family are expected to have the best interests of the individual members in view whenever they make choices for the whole family. Nevertheless, any decision that is good for the family is seen to be a sound decision; how it affects the individual is of secondary importance.

Not all Hindu people live in this traditional way, of course. Modernity and secularization have influenced higher caste Hindu families significantly. The secularization of Hindu families should always be understood to be along a continuum from *beginning to be secularized* to *very secularized*, with the majority of non-traditional families falling somewhere in the middle. Many of these families live in and around the major cities such as New Delhi, Mumbai, Bangalore, Hyderabad, Ahmedabad, Kolkata, and Chennai. They may also live in smaller cities or even villages that have been impacted by the NRI (or nonresident Indian) community who come and go every year, bringing secularization with them.

Secularization has affected the Hindu family in a unique way. Hindus who live in this type of family context intentionally seek to distance themselves from traditionalism because they have rejected the conservative Hindu orthodoxy of their elders. For them, traditional culture isolates and narrows people's lives. Members of these families are increasingly conversant in English, because the parents have been educated in English-language schools and universities. Both parents and children are also very tech savvy. It is now common knowledge that India is a major player in the global high-tech world.

Contemporary India's secularized families may have significantly redefined what it means to be spiritual, often foregoing a meaningful daily worship of deities in their homes and relegating worship to a few special days per year. There is also an escalating trend toward listening to gurus speak on how to be healthy, wealthy, and at peace. More and more, these gurus are looking like corporate CEOs rather than the sadhus and other "holy men" of the past. Furthermore, many young Hindus in large cities have become agnostics, and others have even become atheists. This is a reactionary point of view away from rote religious observance and blind faith.

Perhaps the most significant change that secularization has brought is decentralization from a large extended family to a nuclear family structure that allows for more individuality. For example, many secularized young adults do not give their elders the right to select a mate for them, practicing what is referred to as a "love marriage," or falling in love and getting married, as opposed to having an arranged marriage. Among the highly secularized families, there is also growing disregard for marriage within one's caste. Young people are increasingly free to marry without reference to caste, as long as each family is similarly educated, financially comparable, and equally secular. From this approach, *class* becomes more important than *caste*. Young married couples are also free to live on their own—in a different city, if they wish—and define for themselves how they will relate to their relatives as they pursue career opportunities in the modernizing urban economy.

If the secularized generations financially support their parents and come home from time to time, all will be well and the elders will be willing to overlook almost everything else. But if they fail to show up for festivals and other important occasions, or if they do not consider it necessary to support their parents, the larger family interprets this behavior as an abandonment of Hindu values and an embracing of individualism. Individualism is seen as an offensive Western ideal and frequently causes painful conflict within families. Secularization is not yet the norm for the Hindu civilization, but it is on the rise and does have an impact on culture in modern India.

Traditional or secular, the Hindu family often changes significantly when it settles in the West. Immigrant families often feel that these changes are irresistible and inevitable, something that simply happens to them and is quite beyond their control. Many Hindus eventually come to believe that their family is actually threatened by Western culture and values. Traditional families sometimes experience devastating culture shock that can last for an entire generation as parents and grandparents witness the ignorance, disregard, or even contempt that children have for their values. The children may eventually give up much or all of the traditional Hindu culture their elders hold so dear.

This agonizing culture shock is not bias or prejudice, and it is not really the loss of culture that is breaking the hearts of the older generations. It is the loss of *family*, the loss of *identity*, and the sense that they are being forgotten, even rejected and abandoned. It is not so much pride as it is *grief*. This is often not handled well because it is emotionally overwhelming; it is too much to deal with. For that matter, even when young secularized families come to the West, they can be initially overwhelmed by the individualism they encounter. The emphasis on personal responsibility, rather than the involvement of the community, and the impersonal nature of interactions in the Western world can be disturbing at first.

Any consideration of how the gospel is given and received in a Hindu context must include a clear and realistic understanding of how the family shapes the lives of Hindu people. By the same token, it must also include an awareness of how, increasingly, the individual shapes the life of the family. This family-based and family-focused culture is critical for us to understand, because when Hindu people begin to pray to Jesus, the families will think that they are becoming so westernized or secularized that they are now even becoming *Christians*. As we will see, making disciples in the Hindu context is a *family* affair.

CASTE

The word *caste* is derived from the Portuguese *casta*, meaning lineage, race, or breed. The Portuguese used it to describe the communal dynamics they encountered as they attempted to colonize parts of India in the sixteenth century. The word is now part of the global English lexicon, and it is also embedded in the officially recognized Indian dialect of English.

Even though caste is universally accepted as an appropriate descriptor of Hindu social culture, it does not fully explain how Hindu society is arranged or how it functions. Hindus themselves use the words *varna* and *jati*. *Varna* is the overarching Hindu concept of class, and *jati* means a group of people who are born into the same closed community.

There are four *varnas* of Hindu people. These classes are arranged from higher to lower, and each has a function in traditional Hindu society. The functions are no longer hard and fast, but they are still somewhat relevant to the everyday lives of common people. The highest *varna* are the Brahmins, or priests. Next come the Kshatriyas, who are the royalty and warriors. Below them are the Vaishyas, or traders, businessmen, and landowning farmers. And lowest on this ladder are the Sudras, or laborers. This is the traditional way to conceive of caste in the larger sense.

Modern India uses another set of categories as well: Forward Caste, Other Backward Caste, Scheduled Caste, and Scheduled Tribe. These designations have to do with seats in college and quotas for government jobs being reserved for people from castes that have historically been discriminated against. The Brahmins, Kshatriyas, and Vaishyas are considered Forward Caste, and there is great diversity about how Sudras fit into the quota system for jobs and college admissions.

No one really knows quite how many Hindus nationwide are Forward Caste, and especially how many are Sudras. But the caste categories are quite clear in local contexts, where people pay careful attention to who's who, so to speak. Even though caste is exceedingly difficult to identify nationwide, there are very clear lines of distinction between who is hearing the gospel in India and the diaspora and who is not. The higher a family is within this *varna* culture, the less opportunity they have to hear the gospel.

Varna is the big-picture construct of Hindu social culture, but it is not nearly as important as one's *jati*. Hindu social culture, especially in small towns and villages, is powerfully circumscribed by membership in a *jati*. A *jati* is a specific caste or sub-caste, and every Hindu in the world belongs to one. There are thousands upon thousands of *jatis* because there are millions upon millions of Hindus. Dalits live in *jatis*, but they do not possess *varna* and were in the past contemptuously referred to as "outcastes."

A person's *jati* is often delineated, at least to some extent, by their last name, which means that *jati* is actually all about family and identity and belonging. The relationship between *jati* and identity is so strong because Hindu *jatis* are completely closed social and cultural communities that people enter exclusively through birth. This has made *jati* nearly as personally meaningful as ethnicity. As a result, many Hindus have traditionally seen *jati* as a foundational human endowment, similar to being born French rather than English, or Korean rather than Japanese.

Jati is such a powerful element of how Hindus perceive their identity that we may interpret *jatis* as distinct people groups, especially with regard to Hindus who are more traditional, and especially those who live in or are from villages and small towns. Gospel witnessing movements obviously accept the importance of ethnicity and people groups, and they rightly advocate shaping gospel ministry according to the dynamic context that these communities live within and create. This is sound missiology, and applying it to the Hindu caste context will greatly help the spread of the gospel among them.

The vertical arrangement of the caste system, from higher to lower, has caused all of the power and affluence of Hindu society to be localized almost exclusively among the higher castes, resulting in oppressive poverty and marginalization of the lower castes. Yet in other respects caste has changed considerably since India gained independence in 1947, and it continues to change rapidly as the nation has been confronting modernity in the new millennium. It is likely that the entire notion of caste will become impossible to define in the years to come.

THE CHURCH IN INDIA

India has a vibrant and spiritually rich Christian community that blesses the entire world. There have been Christians in India for nineteen centuries, which means that Christianity has a longer history in this country than it does in most of Europe and certainly far longer than in the Americas. Christianity is an integral and indigenous part of the fascinating diversity of India just as much as any other religion or culture, and it should have a significant claim on the hearts and minds of Indians. In fact, in several states in northeastern India, as well as in the southern state of Kerala, Christianity is mainstream and quite influential. Christianity is also becoming mainstream in the southern states of Andhra Pradesh and Tamil Nadu.

The Indian church is also working vigorously and skillfully to bring the gospel to many non-Christian people. The zeal and commitment of Indian Christians to serve the Lord in some of the most difficult environments is among the very best examples of the apostolic missionary tradition, and God is blessing their labors as thousands of new churches emerge all over the nation. The North American church should be humbled by the example of its Indian counterpart in this regard and seek to emulate their work of faith. Nevertheless, the higher castes continue to receive comparatively little focused gospel ministry in India. There are many valid reasons for this; it's a complex situation and we don't intend to judge it at all, let alone negatively.

The Indian church has come to believe that Hindu civilization and global Christianity are ultimately incompatible, and in many ways Christian experience in India, particularly since Independence, seems to prove that assumption. For example, the Christian community in most parts of the country has had to adapt its ministry philosophy to avoid the real dangers of violent persecution on the one hand and smothering discrimination on the other. The church has also learned to articulate and draw clear lines of ideological and social distinction so their identity as a legitimate community of faith in Jesus Christ remains sharp and unambiguous. These distinctions have served the growing Christian community in India well over many, many years, enabling them to remain a full and honored member of the global Christian communion—Protestant, Catholic, and Orthodox.

An unintended consequence of these clarifying distinctions has been the separation of Christian cultures and people from the non-Christian cultures and people of the land, making appropriate outreach toward higher caste Hindu communities even more challenging than it would be otherwise. Another contributing factor in this separation is the unavoidable fact of life within caste-conscious India: segregation of peoples is a foundational aspect of the Indian worldview.

It is our belief, however, that Christ reigns over Hindu civilization and wants to redeem it and gift it to the world for his glory. Furthermore, we also believe that Hindus who follow Christ apart from membership in the established Indian churches are free to do so, and that they are as much a part of the body of Christ as any Christian family anywhere on earth.

मार्ग

CHAPTER 2

OBSTACLES AND APPROACHES

MANY CHRISTIANS who participate in the global gospel conversation often come to realize that gospel witness on the non-Christian edge is very different from what they may have experienced in their local church-based ministries. Ministry in growing churches and so-called megachurches is designed primarily for the ongoing discipleship of Christian families who are members of that church. This is the core concept of membership in such churches. Some will go a step further and extend their ministry to the people around them who are lapsed in terms of church participation. These churches usually try to attract lapsed Christians into their congregation, so they create a worship and teaching experience that accomplishes that end. A smaller number of churches try to attract non-Christians into their midst. All of these philosophies of ministry are church-based, programmatic, and very successful when done properly.

Nevertheless, none of this good work is applicable to ministry in a totally non-Christian atmosphere. Almost all of us who come from church-based ministry, either in local churches or in focused discipleship ministry organizations, will face a disorienting learning curve if we try to bring the gospel to people who are outside the church and on the gospel edge. Ministry in a Hindu context is like this.

Paradoxical as it might sound, in some ways ministry to Hindus outside the church is easier than ministry to people who are within the church. One reason for this is that Hindus have usually not been inoculated with a tiny bit of Christianity, which makes people immune to the real thing (as E. Stanley Jones observed long ago; see Jones 1925, 119). This "immunization," unfortunately prevalent in an alarming number of Christians around the world, is sometimes referred to as nominal or cultural Christianity. For example, American evangelicalism is currently in a major transition, and almost everyone is dealing with it, reading about it, and discussing it. One example of trying to deal with this cultural Christianity is the resurgence of Reformed theology, which is contextualized to Millennials and their desperate Christian parents. This type of ministry is designed to purify a culturally Christian church. Hindus, on the other hand, are totally beyond these movements, because they are not nominal Christians who resist discipleship.

In other ways, ministry outside the church is harder than ministry in the Christian center. The person ministering on the kingdom edge will soon begin to feel isolated from all of this positive evangelical energy that has encompassed everyone they know. Even the so-called missional movement, which is more incarnational, contextualized, and mission-shaped, often functions within the vacuum left by the departure of the church from the center of Western culture. By contrast, the church has *never* been at the center of Hindu civilization. None of the missional blogs apply to the lives of people on mission in a Hindu context. The realization that we are, in a way, "on our own" usually happens quickly; but it takes much longer for this discovery to move away from being a source of discouragement and confusion about life and ministry, and become transformed into a passionate and determined quest to follow Jesus to this mission frontier. This is certainly the case in ministry with higher caste Hindus.

The difficulties seem to revolve around issues that are not clear to the disciple of Christ, but which somehow make complete sense to Hindus. The disciple will invariably have answers to questions that Hindus never ask—and questions about answers that Hindus inevitably give! For instance, the disciple often refers to salvation and faith and truth, all individually conceived of and received. Hindus, on the other hand, often reflect on *lifestyle* and *karma* and *culture*, all conceived of and received in the context of family and community. Even if the Christian disciple and the Hindus do eventually reach unanimity on both the questions and the answers, the disciple finds that their Hindu friends usually reject the call to convert to Christianity, even though the witness is clear and shared with love and respect. The rejection may be subtle and nonconfrontational, but it will be real.

At this point, discouragement may set in very deeply, and the disciple will become exhausted, confused, sad, and even filled with grief. The vast majority of people who experience this fruitlessness in their witness are not frustrated by a sense of failure to participate in the global triumph of Christianity, for triumphalists cannot survive long in a ministry in which they appear to fail. Instead, the pain is similar to being friends with people who need what we have been freely given, but who either won't accept that they need it or who won't accept it *from us*. This experience will shape the disciple. They will either realize that changes are needed and make adjustments accordingly, or they will decide to never allow themselves to go through this again and walk away. Entire theological systems have been created trying to deal with this reality.

Why do higher caste Hindu people consistently refuse to formally confess Christ? The reason is actually quite obvious, but it is often hard for disciples of Christ to accept. Quite simply, *Hindus aren't Christians*. I don't mean this in a negative or judgmental way. There have certainly been mainstream Hindus who converted to Christianity and became fully Christian. There are also notable examples of Hindus who have received Christ and lived as his disciples from a Hindu perspective. I am not implying that they are somehow "other" or of a secondary status in the kingdom of God. I simply mean that higher caste Hindus are separate from the indigenous Indian Christianity that has existed for centuries in Kerala.

Higher caste Hindus are also separate from the Christendom-based diaspora of churches that were planted across South Asia by godly, dedicated missionaries (both Indian and Western) beginning in the early eighteenth century. Hindus are not part of the Christian community and are thus non-Christian in this sense. On his insightful blog, *Learning India* (learningindia.in), Neil Miller succinctly points out how religion and community are linked: "Religion and India go hand in hand, but remember that in India religion first means community and only later means beliefs."

The significance of this in relation to how complicated gospel witness to Hindus can be is obvious. The majority of the people around the world who share the gospel with Hindus were born into a family that is culturally Christian rather than culturally Muslim or Hindu or Shinto or secular. Moreover, they have experienced Christ within the diverse expressions of cultural or biblical Christianity, including the Catholic Church, the various Protestant denominations, the Orthodox churches, and the many different types of independent Christian churches. *Almost all of the witness to Hindus comes from people who are from these global centers of cultural Christianity.* But Hindus are not connected to this world of Christianity, and that is why Christians find witness to Hindus confusing or even frustrating. The Hindu worldview, collective memory, shared values, history, literature, and religion is non-Christian and non-European. This is why Hindus are *not Christians.*

The implication of this is that there are huge obstacles between Hindus and faith in Jesus. Some of these obstacles are cultural; others are spiritual. Some can be traced back through history; others have arisen in the present and may extend into the future. These obstacles are within people as well as *between* people. They are created by Christians and by Hindus. As we seek to reach higher caste Hindus, we should not only be aware of what these obstacles are, but they must also inform and shape our approach to witness.

OBSTACLE #1:
FOREIGN RELIGION

Christians almost always underestimate how surprising, even shocking, it is for Hindus when they realize the truth of the gospel. The vast majority of Hindus simply do not comprehend that the gospel is good news for *everyone*, regardless of nationality or ethnicity or family background, and it affects them deeply when they realize that Jesus is Lord of all, and his kingdom is universal.

For example, Hindus almost always assign Jesus to the Christian religion; to their mind, he is the "god" of the Christians. Furthermore, they assign Christianity to the Western world, perceiving both as two parts of one civilizational whole. Since Hindus see Christianity as entirely of the West rather than of the world, they naturally believe it is foreign to them, since it has nothing to do with Hindu civilization. And because they do not consider this Christian civilization to be any better than their own, they do not feel any attraction to Jesus; he is lost to them within what they believe is a Christian—and therefore *foreign*—civilization.

There is a valid basis for this point of view. It is true that Christianity has been strongly identified with Western civilization in India because of the legacy of European Christendom, which colonized all of what is today known as South Asia. As Christianity was spread in colonial India by missionaries from Christendom, it frequently took a largely Christendom form. For example, many of the church buildings that emerged in India were almost exactly like those in Europe or North America. For generations the Indian congregations that used these buildings were presided over by Western bishops and missionaries.

At the same time, the Hindu view of Jesus and Christianity also contains a grave error. India-born historian Dr. Robert Frykenberg in his masterwork, *The History of Christianity in India*, points out that it has always been untrue to assume that the Christian West introduced Christianity to India during the colonial period of Indian history. Christianity found a home in India long before it did in England and certainly before it spread to North America. A very popular—and to some, *unquestioned*—tradition is that the apostle Thomas brought the gospel to India in AD 52. This is possible, but hard to prove from history. According to Philip Jenkins, the author of *Lost Christianity*, traders from the Christian Middle East brought Christianity to Kerala, then known as Malabar, perhaps beginning as early as the second century. Historical evidence of "formal church life" in Kerala can be traced to AD 345. It has been thriving in that coastal state for all these centuries and is now indigenous to the local people. Jenkins points out another largely unknown fact: the Nestorian Church (the Church of the East) had assigned a Metropolitan, or a "bishop of bishops," in Patna, capital of the northern state of Bihar, sometime in the thirteenth century.

Nevertheless, many Hindus continue to believe that Christianity is a foreign religion and an incompatible way of life that was brought to India during the colonial period when westerners sought to exploit India. In this matter, perception is reality. Since these same colonialists were so-called Christians who dominated India for well over three centuries, Christianity is identified with coercion and oppression to this day.

OBSTACLE #2: HINDU IDENTITY

When the Holy Spirit reveals the lordship of Christ to Hindus who believe that Christianity is not indigenous to India, they struggle to know how to respond, because they often assume that they must abandon their Hindu identity and assume a Christian identity in order to follow Jesus. For the most part, Hindus do not know if it is possible for them to adopt a lifestyle of devotion and service that is focused exclusively on Jesus; they assume that only Christians can really do that.

This confusion is all about *culture* rather than *religious faith*, and it should not be hard for westerners to understand, because it is very similar to how culture, nationality, and religious faith merge or fail to merge in North America. No one would suggest that a Native American in Oklahoma has to assume Taiwanese immigrant identity in order to become a disciple of Christ. Try telling an English-speaking Canadian that they must become an American in order to be a "real" Christian and watch the sparks fly! In the same way, Hindus do not have to assume a Christian identity to follow Christ. True followers of Christ know that there's much more to being a Christian than adopting a certain culture, but that is primarily how Hindus interpret a call to become a Christian.

This misconception, perhaps more than any other, prevents the gospel from spreading freely within upper caste Hindu communities in India and around the world. In this matter Hindus are both right and wrong. They rightly believe that many people, both Indian and non-Indian, Hindu and Christian, assume that Hindus must convert away from their Hindu identity and assume a Christian identity in order to become disciples of Jesus Christ. And they wrongly assume that this is a *requirement* of faith and central to the gospel.

This situation is very similar to what the early church faced as Gentiles began to hear the gospel and believe in Christ. Jesus, as the Jewish Messiah, was the fulfillment of the prophetic promises to Israel. His virgin birth, his three-year ministry, and his death, resurrection, and ascension happened in Israel, and his original band of disciples were all Jews. When the promised Holy Spirit was initially given, only the Jewish disciples of Jesus were filled. Since Christianity began as a Jewish movement of faith in a Jewish Messiah among the Jewish people, they naturally thought everything with reference to Jesus should be regulated by Jews and their culture. It is worth noting that they ignored the powerful ministry Jesus had done among non-Jews because, as far as we know, these people were not baptized with the Holy Spirit on the Day of Pentecost. However, things began to change rather quickly after that.

When the Gentiles began to believe in Christ and receive the Holy Spirit—who is the Spirit of Christ—in the same manner as the Jews, it soon became clear that Jesus was the Messiah of all, both Jews and Gentiles. However, putting this truth into practice was not without its difficulties. The epistle to the Galatians was written to deliver the truth into these complicated transitions. It laid a foundation of faith and practice within the new Messianic movement that would enable it to become global and multicultural.

Paul, the apostle to the Gentiles, tells the Galatians that they don't need to be circumcised or become Jewish in culture or religious practice in order to receive Christ and live as his disciples. On the contrary, he says that if Gentiles submit to circumcision, they have moved away from the gospel of grace and embraced a false gospel of obeying the Law in order to be accepted by God.

This was really a heart problem as much as it was a theological or missiological one. Simply put, some Messianic Jewish leaders in the early church wanted everybody to live like they did so they could control them like the Pharisees had always done in traditional Jewish culture. They forgot, however, that just a few years before, Jesus had soundly refuted the Pharisees and their oppressive, isolationist dogma. Thus he had wrested the kingdom from their grasp and given it to the common Jewish people—a precursor to ultimately giving it to the world when the Holy Spirit was poured out upon all people everywhere.

That Gentiles did not have to abandon their identity and take on Jewish identity to be followers of Jesus was certainly hard to understand and put into practice, but it was not something new, like an extreme form of contextualization that Paul and Barnabas came up with on their missionary journeys. It was the missional, contextual, and theological application of all that Jesus had said and done for three years in Israel. The epistle to the Galatians built upon the foundation of what Jesus did with Samaritans and Gentiles during his earthly ministry. This teaching was not accepted by everyone, and it is difficult for some groups of Christians to accept even today.

Hindus do not have to abandon their culture or identity as Hindus and take on a Christian identity and culture any more than Gentiles had to assume a Jewish identity and culture, or Mexicans have to become French-speaking Canadians in order to become disciples of Christ. In fact, as Galatians clearly teaches, they should *not* do so, because Christian discipleship is entirely about grace, not about cultural customs. Hindus must not be coerced in any manner to change their cultural identity so they can follow Christ. If they wish to do so, they are free to assume a Christian identity, and the love of Christ demands that Christians fully accept them either way. Requiring a change of identity as a matter of doctrine, however, is "a different gospel," as Paul says in Galatians 1:6.

Nevertheless, Hindu-focused ministry carried out by Christians, be they Indian or foreign, is frequently done in such a way that Hindus are brought to an identity crisis. The choice presented to Hindus is that they must decide between their family or the church, their holidays and dietary customs or Christian ones, and so on. Until Christians understand how to apply the message of Galatians to a Hindu context and stop thrusting Hindus into an identity crisis, millions of Hindus will continue to resist any call to faith in Christ.

OBSTACLE #3: CHRISTIAN IDENTITY

Another obstacle to faith for upper caste Hindu people is the exceedingly sensitive subject of caste and the church. If you are a Christian from India, I beg your indulgence on this. Please forgive any offense my words may cause.

Caste is clearly still an issue for the Indian Christian community. For example, some Christians prefer to belong to churches made up of people who are known to be from their own caste background.

This is a matter of choice. Others are from a part of India where all of the Christians are from the same caste background, so there is no real choice involved.

Apart from being a delicate issue, caste and the church in India can be complex. Hindu people frequently consider all Christians in India to be from the very lowest caste background, now referred to as Dalits. Over the last 150 years or so, many thousands of Dalits have responded to the gospel. Those who are from that background are one body with the entire Christian world. In his seminal book on this subject, *The Dalit Christians: A History*, John C. B. Webster states that approximately 55 percent of the total population of Christians in India are from a Dalit background, which is the majority of Christians in North India (2009). This is the historical background for people movements in India. Because the majority of Indian Christians are Dalits, many caste-conscious Hindus now actually identify *all* Christians as Dalits and use this as the reason for refusing to consider the gospel, for they are unwilling to risk being identified as lower caste.

This issue of Dalits and Christianity in India is complicated, delicate, and controversial. There is a darkness surrounding it that cannot be denied and should not be ignored. By no means do all Hindus feel this way, but most do nothing to challenge the idea. By their silence they tacitly accept the evil of bigotry based on caste discrimination toward Dalits and, by extension, toward Christians. This is a huge problem Christians have to deal with when they consider the call to bring the gospel to every community in India.

OBSTACLE #4:
SPIRITUAL BLINDNESS

Many upper caste Hindus are respectful and fair-minded. They make the best friends and neighbors one could ever have. They work hard, love their children, care for their parents, and seek to live in harmony and goodwill with the larger community around them, be it a Hindu, Muslim, Christian, Sikh, Jain, or Buddhist one. These Hindus are aware of the need for social and economic reform regarding caste within India and are in favor of bringing justice and a greater equality of opportunity to all Indians. People who try to share the gospel in a Hindu society or community will encounter these fair-minded Hindus. If you unashamedly practice your faith and devotion to Jesus with other believers, these Hindus will tolerate it just fine, for they believe in religious freedom and pluralism. But try to witness to them as a friend, sharing what you have experienced of the power of the gospel, and you will begin to see a change in their relationship with you. They may distance themselves from you or let you know in a courteous manner that they have no interest in your personal religious beliefs. You will have to accept that and pray privately for your friends, continuing to enjoy the things that you do have in common with them.

A further and more perplexing change occurs when these friends enter times of need or trial. At such times, if you come alongside them and ask for their permission to pray with them, rarely will they say no. But as Jesus starts answering your prayers, you may see these same people change before your eyes when they realize that Jesus himself is approaching them. They may quickly turn to hate you and even persecute you, simply because you have prayed to God for them in the name of Jesus and Jesus has provided for them. It is amazing how that happens.

Sometimes this change happens because we are triumphalistic: we translate Jesus into their lives with strings attached because we want to change them. It's that same Galatian problem again. Sometimes, however, the believer simply wants to ask God to help their friends who are in need, and he or she knows they can only do so in Jesus' name. And because Jesus is the living Lord, he answers prayers. This threatens the Hindu people, who then turn against their believing friend.

Why does this happen? Do Hindus hate Jesus? No, the vast majority of Hindus respect Jesus and think highly of him. However, *Satan* hates Jesus, and because Jesus loves all people, including Hindus, Satan hates *them* as well. Hindus don't know this, but it is true. When they discover that Satan hates everyone on earth, including themselves, it can make them feel singled out and hurt them deeply. We must therefore be very careful how we communicate this truth, lest we give the offensive and mistaken impression that Hinduism is thoroughly satanic. Hinduism is no more or less satanic than any of the other *isms* that claim the minds and hearts of people around the world—including Christless Christianity, the practice of Christianity without an emphasis on a personal relationship of surrender to Jesus Christ.

Satan has absolutely no power over Jesus, because Jesus completely overpowered him when he died on the cross and rose again. Knowing his impotence to fight Jesus, Satan deceives people about Jesus. This is sometimes referred to as spiritual blindness. The apostle Paul powerfully explains how Satan deceives people by blinding their spiritual eyes to the truth of Jesus Christ:

> Therefore, since through God's mercy we have this ministry, we do not lose heart. Rather, we have renounced secret and shameful ways; we do not use deception, nor do we distort the word of God. On the contrary, by setting forth the truth plainly we commend ourselves to everyone's conscience in the sight of God. And even if our gospel is veiled, it is veiled to those who are perishing. The god of this age has blinded the minds of unbelievers, so that they cannot see the light of the gospel that displays the glory of Christ, who is the image of God. (2 Cor 4:1–6)

It is critical to understand exactly what this scripture is saying. It tells us that Satan tries to prevent *all* people, not just Hindus, from understanding who Jesus is. His evil work is described as spiritually blinding us so we cannot really see Jesus. Satan deceives us so we cannot grasp the reality of the person and work of Jesus, making us unable to personalize what that means for us and those we know. This satanic blinding is why your otherwise loyal and loving Hindu friends may abandon you or even turn on you if Jesus begins to work in their lives.

Satan is selective about those he blinds. He doesn't blind open-minded people who are struggling to understand and believe. Nor does he blind those who don't yet understand and believe. He doesn't even blind people who may be confused and antagonistic. He only blinds *unbelievers*, deceiving them until they begin to develop a determined unwillingness to believe. In other words, those who won't believe eventually *can't* believe.

Nevertheless, the passage of Scripture quoted above does not suggest that we fall into hopeless despair about unbelievers. We can actually work together with God and continue to share the gospel with all people, even those who are being blinded by Satan. As Paul continues,

> For what we preach is not ourselves, but Jesus Christ as Lord, and ourselves as your servants for Jesus' sake. For God, who said, "Let light shine out of darkness," made his light shine in our hearts to give us the light of the knowledge of God's glory displayed in the face of Christ. (2 Cor 4:5–6)

God, who spoke light into existence when darkness covered everything (Gen 1:2), can do the same for any person or group of people in the world. The gospel is the content of the creative word of God, who can "speak" faith into existence as he spoke creation into existence. We must never think that this person or that group of people are blinded by Satan beyond all hope. We don't know who is totally blinded due to their determined unbelief, and we should not concern ourselves with that. We must focus on living in union with Christ so we may be his voice when he speaks the faith-creating word of the gospel to Hindu people.

This concludes our examination of the major obstacles higher caste Hindus face with respect to understanding and accepting the gospel of Christ. Now let us turn to the approaches we must take as we seek to witness to this group of people.

APPROACH #1:
CONTEXTUALIZATION

Contextualization is the adapting of the gospel message to the current political, religious, economic, and cultural way of life of a given group of people, so that the communication retains its clarity and speaks to the situation that people actually face. When it is done well, those who are on the receiving end of contextualized ministry will realize that Jesus is the good news they have been waiting to hear. They will then begin to believe that his lordship can restore, redeem, or deliver them. Contextualization is often necessary when believers begin to bring Jesus to Hindu families. Consider what Paul has to say on this:

> Though I am free and belong to no one, I have made myself a slave to everyone, to win as many as possible. To the Jews I became like a Jew, to win the Jews. To those under the law I became like one under the law (though I myself am not under the law), so as to win those under the law. To those not having the law I became like one not having the law (though I am not free from God's law but am under Christ's law), so as to win those not having the law. To the weak I became weak, to win the weak. I have become all things to all people so that by all possible means I might save some. I do all this for the sake of the gospel, that I may share in its blessings. (1 Cor 9:19–23)

It is perfectly right to add "to the Hindus I became like a Hindu, to win the Hindus." This is by no means dangerous and controversial, but is instead the clear teaching of Scripture. The Bible, not human tradition or opinion, is God's final authoritative word on how we conduct ourselves and our ministries. As those who claim to live under the rule of Jesus as revealed in Scripture, we do not have the freedom to disregard what Paul says in this passage by refusing to contextualize our ministry to Hindus. To do so is ignorance at best and pharisaical at worst.

We often hear that a simple sharing of the gospel is all that is needed to fulfill our role in bringing Jesus to Hindus, but this is not at all biblical. Jesus was a master communicator—he was *the* master communicator—and he understood those to whom he preached extremely well. He knew how they spent their time, what they valued, what they ate and drank, and how they worshipped and married and celebrated and did business. He also knew who they loved and who they hated. This knowledge informed what Jesus taught and how he taught it. He believed in communicating the gospel he had received from his Father in ways that made sense to the Jewish people he loved.

Apart from what the Gospels tell us about Jesus' ministry methods, the book of Acts also shows us that Paul and Barnabas were skilled in understanding culture, language, philosophy, and rhetoric as they traveled the Roman Empire preaching the gospel. They did not embrace ignorance as a ministry philosophy but worked all their lives to understand the people to whom they preached, so they could "by all means save some."

APPROACH #2:
CONTEXTUAL SKILLS

What follows is a list of contextual skills that ministry within a Hindu context may require. They are listed in ascending order, from the most basic and easiest to acquire, to the more difficult ones.

Learn to say each person's entire name correctly. Hindus often adjust the pronunciation of their names to sound more westernized (or they may even use a Western name), because westerners cannot or will not learn how to say their actual name. If a Westerner pronounces a Hindu person's name correctly, it resonates within the heart of the Hindu family, because they know their names take an effort to learn. Many Hindus have smiled and thanked me when I pronounced their name correctly the second time we met.

Learn to appreciate Indian food and participate in the Hindu food culture. Hindus value their food and their food customs highly. A sign outside a large Indian grocery store near my house pithily captures this attitude: "Celebrating our food and our culture." Many Hindus are vegetarian, and Western believers will endear themselves to Hindu families if they show an interest in learning how to cook and eat Indian food. I must admit, this is the best part of ministry to Hindus!

Learn to develop Hindu forms of courtesy and politeness. This centers around relationship formalities and giving and receiving respect. Some examples include removing shoes inside the house, not letting your feet make contact with people, displaying respectful courtesy to older people, and controlling your emotions—especially the negative ones. Hindu people respect and value even-temperedness. As we minister to Hindus, we must relearn discretion—something that the Western culture no longer values.

Learn how the Hindu family structure works. The Hindu family is paternal, with older men as leaders. Relationships are based on following certain formalities. Informal family life takes place only if formal family life is followed. Each family has their own interpretation of these formalities, so they vary from family to family. What does not vary is the fact that a person simply cannot live within a family without following them. Therefore, discipleship of believers from a Hindu background must include an understanding of this very important aspect of Hindu life.

Learn about Hindu deities and worship forms. Nearly every Hindu family has a small *mandir*, or temple, in their house. Within the temple are small idols or pictures of various gods and goddesses. They will explain it all to you if you ask, but make sure you ask in an appropriately respectful manner, without sounding too inquisitive, and at the right time. Don't make it the first thing you ask them when you enter their home. And when they start explaining it to you, try to use it as an opportunity to find out more about their spiritual beliefs. This will give you a better idea of where that particular person is and how to pray for and minister to them specifically.

Learn about Hindu festivals. As you set about learning their religious calendar, make sure you use the word "festival" and not "holiday," which they use as Americans use "vacation." The most important Hindu festival is Diwali; others are Dussera, Nav Ratri, Holi, Janmastami, Pongal, and Durga Pooja. Some are celebrated nationally, others regionally. There are a number of other festivals as well, but these are the most important ones. When believers are invited to participate in Hindu holidays, there can be some uncertainty about what will happen because the believer does not want to inadvertently worship a deity other than Jesus. This might make the believer hold back rather than joining in the celebration. However, these situations are wonderful opportunities to show Hindus that Jesus is not an enemy of their culture. Ask God to guide you, and feel free to participate to the extent that the Holy Spirit leads. If you are sure that a certain act is considered to be worship, then politely decline participating in it. Your hosts will have no problem with that. If you are not sure, then go forward and participate, entrusting yourself to God's grace. If you find out later that you have erred, do not fear. The Hindus will not react against you, and God knows our hearts. Learn from the experience and develop ways to adjust. As far as possible, however, try to find out as much as you can beforehand so you know what to expect.

Learn about Hindu holy scriptures and philosophy. Their main scripture is the Bhagavad Gita, and next in importance are the Vedas, the Upanishads, the Ramayana, and the Mahabharata. Various mythologies are also included among the sacred writings of the Hindu religion. Most Hindus have not read them but are familiar with the stories, just as most westerners have never read the Bible but may be familiar, say, with the story of David and Goliath. Regarding Hindu philosophy, there is huge diversity of opinions and beliefs, and it may not be applicable unless the people bring it up. In fact, it may be best to leave philosophy alone, because this sidetracks the conversation and leads nowhere.

Learn the language. I admit, this is the biggest and most time-consuming commitment to make. It may be impossible to become fluent in an Indian language, but even a few words can be helpful and open doors to people's hearts. Begin by learning greetings, how to say please and thank you, how to compliment a hostess for a meal, how to thank someone for a favor, and even how to ask for help. It is a compliment to someone when you ask to learn their language as they have learned (or are learning) yours. Ask them to teach you, and it can be mutually beneficial, heartwarming, and bridge-building.

APPROACH #3:
BUILDING A WITNESS

Perhaps the most important thing I have learned about contextualizing the gospel to higher caste Hindus is that an effective witness is something that must be built over time. Being an evangelist, I was used to a straightforward gospel throw-down, which worked well in the combat discipleship context of non–Bible Belt North America. This was, however, woefully inappropriate for a Hindu context, where I learnt that we must spend time building a witness that connects meaningfully to Hindus. There are three major reasons for this.

First, building a witness means accepting the effect of culture on gospel communication. Communication theory assumes that clarity of presentation will lead to understanding. A communicator must therefore be able to function fully within the cultural expectations of the people to whom he or she is communicating, in order for the message to be understood most fully. When I began ministry to upper caste Hindus, I did not yet appreciate the significant difference between witness as an insider to other North Americans with whom I had almost complete communication affinity, and witness as a non-Hindu, non-Indian person to Hindus from India, with whom I had almost no affinity. I had to learn how to build a witness rather than assume that I already had one. This is actually an issue of humility.

Second, we must build a contextualized witness to Hindus because of the common misunderstandings and misconceptions that many Hindus have about Jesus. These can be major obstacles to witness, and Hindu people will inevitably have to deal with them as they journey toward faith. A higher caste Gujarati woman once told me that Jesus was born in London approximately two centuries ago, as the English-speaking incarnation of the Hindu god Krishna. She had no idea about the death and resurrection of Jesus Christ or his gift of eternal life. In fact, she knew almost nothing true about Jesus, and she was completely convinced of facts that were remarkably *untrue* about him. Behind that intelligent woman's point of view is an entire worldview of ideas about religion, civilization, and British colonialism that is quite common to Indians. Almost all higher caste Hindus have a point of view about Jesus that includes a mixture of truth, error, and ignorance.

Third, building a witness to Hindus is essential because Hindus build a response to him *over time*. They rarely receive him as Savior and Lord right away. The paradigm-breaking truth is that Hindus themselves actually build a positive response to the gospel that is centered on *practice* rather than *knowledge*. Instead of internalizing the claims and concepts of the propositional gospel idea as a foundation upon which to convert to Christianity, a Hindu person or family will usually feel compelled to deepen and clarify their experience with Jesus, most often by participating in Christ-centered worship and prayer. They are equally open to Bible study and maintaining a relationship with believers in Christ. By being among Christians in this manner, they begin to build a positive response to

Jesus. Thus, our building a fruitful and faithful witness to Hindus that coincides with their building a positive and deepening response to Jesus is the essential skill to be learned. Eventually, our witness and their response become two parts of one organic whole.

As Hindus and Christians pray, worship, study the Bible, and witness together, they all walk on a path of spiritual discovery and of deeper acceptance and surrender to a reality that they might never have dreamed to be true. For a Hindu family, this will enable them to say, "Jesus is indeed Lord, eternal life is indeed in his name, and we as a Hindu family can embrace him as our Savior and Lord and follow him according to our ancient culture and identity."

KETAN'S STORY

We initially met Ketan (not his real name) and his family in a small town in eastern New Jersey, through a cricket match organized by his son. A group of Indian teenagers would frequently gather in the parking lot of our office building to play after school, because they all lived in nearby apartment buildings and this lot was usually only partially full. Around three in the afternoon we would hear the boys yelling at each other, and we would walk outside to watch them play, assuring them that it was okay for them to gather there.

A relationship gradually developed between us and a group of about ten boys. They were classic immigrants who lived multicultural lives. They had all been born in India and had moved to the US as children. None of them were wealthy, but their parents knew how to handle money very well, so they always had enough. The parents spoke various levels of English in public, but never at home. All of the families lived as closely as possible to the life they had led in India, a way of life they longed for even as they taught their children to take full advantage of the economic opportunity that had originally brought them to the US. The people who lived in these buildings and neighborhoods were not all doctors, engineers, or IT professionals. While those Indians in those professions have steadily migrated to the US, the Indian immigrant community also includes many who are less educated and less modern. The family of Ketan, who was pursuing business opportunities in this country, was one such.

One day Ketan's son invited us to come over to meet his family, so my wife and I arranged to meet him outside his apartment after work. The building was five stories high, and about forty Indian families lived there. The delightful aroma of North Indian vegetarian cooking greeted us as we walked into the building. We could hear Hindi music in the hallways, and after a moment we became conscious of the stares of the other residents, who had instantly sensed that we didn't belong there. They weren't hostile; they were just curious.

When we entered Ketan's apartment, we felt we had left America behind. The family lived as closely as they could to how they had lived in India. They greeted us and showed us hospitality in a typically Indian way, leaving us sitting in the living room as they served us water, followed by some spicy, crunchy snack and, of course, chai.

It seemed that God had prepared for us to be in relationship with Ketan and his family, because we hit it off right away. Over the next few months we helped them improve their English, worked on our apartments together, and ate together. We basically did life together—and genuinely enjoyed it. Ketan had a large extended family living nearby, totaling around fifty people. We went to their homes and met them all. Whenever anybody arrived from India or from out of town, Ketan would bring them to our apartment. It was remarkable to these people that my wife, Melanie, could make authentic chai.

During Hindu holidays or special occasions such as Diwali or Nav Ratri, we would meet the families of the other boys who played cricket with Ketan's son and see to what extent Ketan's family was connected to these other people. Several of the men in Ketan's family were very successful businessmen, and we would go with him to their stores or factories and learn about what they were doing. He brought us inside a very wide world, often closed to outsiders, and introduced us to numerous Hindu families. In Luke 10, Jesus tells his disciples to look for and connect with a "person of peace," and Ketan was that man for us. Thanks to him, we were swept into the huge Hindu community in our area.

In all of our relationships with Hindus, we were very plain and open about Jesus and all he had done for us. We did not hide the centrality of Jesus in our lives, nor did we retreat from acting as we would around people who may have already been believers. We were ourselves, with just a bit of discretion included. (As a side note, this has always translated well to non-Christians, but not so well to conservative Christians, because then we no longer meet *their* expectations. I suppose we must live with that.)

We refrained from trying to persuade these people to accept Christ as their Lord and Savior. This was counterintuitive for the evangelist in me, but we somehow knew deep down that a prescriptive evangelism approach would be a big mistake. We know now that our sincere evangelism efforts would have almost certainly been interpreted as an egotistical, self-serving insistence that they become something that was more acceptable to us; in other words, it would communicate to them that they must abandon their Hindu identity, receive Christ as their Lord and Savior, and embrace a Christian identity.

We brought Jesus to them in word and deed, but made no effort to bring *them* to *Jesus* by trying to convert them. As a result, they accepted us and our Jesus-centered way of life and did not feel at all uncomfortable around us. We prayed daily for them, asking God to somehow reveal the lordship of Jesus to them and also give us opportunities to share the gospel more deeply. As it turns out, this is always a wise approach, and the apostle Paul sought prayer for the same thing. In Colossians 4:3–4 he asks the believers to pray that he will have opportunities to preach the gospel and for clarity in his speaking.

One day, as Ketan and I were sitting on the stoop outside his apartment building, he suddenly began telling me about his problems. These were considerable, but I already knew a lot of the story anyway. I told him very simply that Jesus would forgive all his sin. Ketan seemed surprised to hear that Jesus would forgive him. As we sat there and discussed the death and resurrection of Christ, Ketan radiated a desire to know more. Kindled on his face was a flame of hope—the hope of forgiveness. Some minutes later, right there on the stoop of his building, Ketan prayed to Christ for forgiveness. He did that because he trusted me.

To be honest, I was shocked. The simplicity of Ketan's confession to Christ of his wrongdoing and his request for forgiveness surprised me. I did not know how to interpret this, so I waited, and I watched.

As time went on, it became clear that God had done a real work in Ketan's life. He had been forgiven, and he knew it. Many other people saw it too. They saw a self-controlled humility and teachableness emerge in his life that was remarkably attractive and appealing, quite different from his usual approach to life. Everyone assumed that our friendship had had something to do with this, because Melanie and I were thought to be people of high moral character who were conscious of God, and our friendship with Ketan's family was seen to be a fortunate boon for the family.

When others Hindus eventually heard that Ketan had asked Jesus to forgive his sins and had begun to pray to him, they were simply—and quite naturally—confused and surprised rather than shocked and outraged. There was no attempt to cut us off from the family or to "reconvert" Ketan. He simply said that he prayed to Jesus now. We had never judged anyone for praying to their traditional gods, so *he* never did. We had lived Christ-centered lives within this family and so Ketan thought he should too, without any attempt to convince anyone to join him. His way of life had been so positively affected that everyone was satisfied with the arrangement.

I met with him in his living room several times a week. We would read the Bible and pray while other people sat around and listened.

Eventually, Ketan became a bold witness for Jesus within his Hindu world, telling people everywhere that he was now praying to Jesus Christ and had become a new man. The changes in his life, and the new joy in his family, were irrefutable evidence that something really good was happening to him, so the Hindu community did not openly oppose this. The news about Jesus and his love and power was spreading in a very Hindu way. In other words, a story, a narrative, of the transformation that Jesus had brought about in Ketan's life was being told all over town without any attempt to formalize or doctrinalize it, because Hindus themselves were telling the story.

Furthermore, it seemed that no one was upset. In fact, people wanted to hear the story of how Ketan began praying to Jesus. Many people were talking about his faith in Christ, and how only good things were the result. Even people in India heard about it and the way we had blessed the family. Frequent invitations to dinner further expanded our influence. No one else was joining Ketan in his new faith, but a door for the gospel to be communicated had been opened wide. So we began to walk through that door.

Yogesh (not his real name) and his family lived upstairs from Ketan. They were from a rural area of India, and life in America was hard for them. As a result, Yogesh had several problems and his family was disintegrating. He was friends with Ketan and had heard from him about his new way of life and how he now prayed to Jesus. Yogesh told his wife, who then invited us to their apartment. "I love your God!" she said when we went to visit them. This was her expression of a desire to worship Jesus and to entreat him on behalf of her struggling family.

Hindus assume that Jesus will accept their worship, and he does. As they worship him, he starts revealing himself to them, lovingly and patiently drawing them to embrace him as Lord. It is a true relational approach to Jesus, like falling in love with him or idolizing him as your hero. It is not conversion based on doctrine.

Ketan began to meet with Yogesh and his wife, and in his own way share his new life with them. Once as we were with them in their apartment, Yogesh told us about a group of twelve men who would meet under a tree in his hometown in India to worship what he referred to as the true God, nameless and without an image. Yogesh and his wife thought we were representatives of this god.

We regularly gathered at Ketan's house for prayer and Bible study. The extended family would come to sing songs and hear the Bible reading. We would discuss the scriptures, trying to make them understandable and clear. We would always share prayer requests and ask God in the name of Jesus to answer our petitions. Those who attended these gatherings would ask us to help them in certain spiritual ways. For example, we were invited to bless new business ventures and new babies in the name of Jesus. We began to find that these people had many, many problems and secret sins that they were starting to confess to us and to Jesus, seeking forgiveness. It was all completely different from any local church ministry we had ever experienced. It was highly experiential and relational within in a totally non-Christian environment.

We eventually discovered that there was a significant minority of Hindu people who opposed this Christ-centered change in Ketan's life and his transparent gospel ministry, but many more were thrilled to see the transformation, so those who opposed us had little power to stop it. We felt like we were on the verge of a real breakthrough. We were thrilled and hopeful, filled with confidence and expecting great things to happen. Instead, we were soon to see everything break down.

✳ ✳ ✳ ✳ ✳

Business had always been the bane of Ketan's existence. The pressure and stress of owning and operating a business had long threatened to destroy his life and family. Everyone he knew was a business owner and was thriving financially, though their personal lives were sinful and empty. In many ways it was his failure in business that had softened his heart to receive Christ in such a compelling and childlike manner. Satan, knowing the stranglehold of business, saw a chance in this area and pounced.

One day some men approached Ketan and tried to get him involved as a partner in a business. This in itself was not an evil plan, but rather a typical way that people in their circles helped each other. Ketan was tempted to accept, thinking that since he had completely changed he could handle it, but his wife and immediate family were totally opposed to the idea. They wanted him to simply work for a living within the extended family businesses, being content to pray to Jesus in a life of simplicity and peace, and many people in his extended family and the local Hindu community were of the same opinion. And Ketan was ready to do this—he was unable to deny how good things were. So Satan sent in the wolves.

Some of the men around him began to mock and harass him. In their view he was a loser because he worked for somebody else and was not a partner in a business. We would sit and discuss this, pointing out how we need to resist the temptation to listen to evil men and instead remain true to Christ. Ketan's family, who were not yet believers, would join in, fully in agreement, telling him that these men had hurt them before and would do it again without remorse.

The way of life and peace was before Ketan. His wife and children were happy to be believers in Jesus. There was a growing movement of Hindu people who felt that they could experience the same type of redemption. He would be a major part of that. God had put a wonderful destiny right in front of him—and sadly, he walked away from it.

Ketan chose to listen to the mockers. Over the next two years we watched him try and fail in business several times, always spiraling into sin, always tearfully repenting, but eventually always listening to the wolves Satan had sent his way.

The movement of people toward Christ eventually stopped because the Hindu people did not see lasting fruit in Ketan's life. It finally became clear that he wanted the praise of these men more than the redemption of Jesus and a happy life with his family. In four years we went from "Break In" to "Break Through" to "Break Down."

What did we learn from this experience? We learned that our ministry within this large community had both strengths and weaknesses, and we have never seen it any other way. Ministry always seems to have both, primarily because people are not perfect—and this includes those who are ministering as well as those who are on the receiving end.

On the one hand, our focus on building relationship with the people and on their experiencing the reality of Jesus was appropriate and effective. This experience, or *anubhav*, of Jesus touched the people's souls, and it is why we feel that we conducted outreach correctly and laid a proper foundation upon which to develop ongoing ministry. However, our major failure was that we did not build *adequately* upon this foundation, because the movement to Christ did not last. Looking back on the experience, we realize that we failed in a number of ways.

First, we failed to create a consistent and contextualized experience of Christ *bhakti*, or worship of Christ, for Ketan, his family, and the Hindu community that was involved in this brief gospel movement. While we had discovered a relational, experiential, and participatory ministry of evangelism, and while the initial discipleship worked well in the Hindu context, we did not fully realize that participatory, experiential worship was needed to further strengthen these people in Christ, and that it should have naturally followed the type of outreach we had begun.

It is true that we met together often in what anyone would describe as a contextualized model of gathering, and in what we assumed was a culturally relevant and biblically faithful manner. However, it was all too culturally neutral in style and feeling. In other words, it was *neither Hindu nor Christian*. It simply did not provide the context for God to speak at the heart level to this entirely Hindu group of people, so obviously they struggled to surrender their hearts to Jesus. Instead, we should have embraced a much more robust form of Hindu discipleship to Jesus. We should have diligently sought out every way possible to worship Jesus in Hindu forms so that Hindus could hear and respond to God at the heart level and be empowered to become disciples of Jesus. We knew we had to adjust, but we completely underestimated quite how much.

Second, as a result of the first mistake, we failed to teach the gospel deeply to the people. Because we had not done a good job at creating an opportunity for contextualized and consistent bhakti for them, our teaching was too westernized and inconsistent, lacking the depth of gospel fullness that was required to establish Ketan and his family in Christ. It did not give them strength to resist temptation or disentangle them from the syncretism that was still frequently evident in their lives.

Third, we failed to establish comfortable and meaningful Hindu forms of worship of Jesus, forms that would speak to their heart, and our mistake in this area was aggravated by our inconsistent teaching of the gospel. This made it virtually impossible to develop an ongoing discipleship ministry to teach them how to live out the fullness of the gospel in the power of the Holy Spirit.

Finally, there is another important point to take from this account, one that should not be overlooked or reduced to a side note. This point is very relevant to our lives to this day and will be for anyone who seeks to translate their experience of Jesus among Hindu families. It is that *we did not take responsibility for the choices that Ketan made.* He had experienced forgiveness and been given a new lease on life. His family and friends supported his walk with Christ—and indeed, many were also beginning to approach Jesus. But when barraged by the forces of hell, Ketan chose, with eyes wide open, to walk away from the love and light of Christ.

Even as I write this now, many years after these events transpired, regret fills my heart. On the one hand, I know deep within that we did our best. I really believe that. I also know that Christ's judgment on this is what really matters, and that judgment will come later, both to us and to them. Christ sees everything fully and his knowledge is perfect, so even though I shudder with fear at the Judge, I trust in his righteous mercy.

My biggest regret has to do with the long-term impact of this ministry. Ketan died recently, and his sons, now wealthy businessmen, called to let me know. They asked us to come over and visit the family. My wife and I went, and it was a joyful and sober reunion with many old friends. I left knowing that Jesus remained a part of the consciousness and faith of this family, even though they had become devotees of a Gujarati god rather than public devotees of Jesus. I know this for a fact because of a request made by Ketan's oldest son, the young cricket-playing boy I had met in the parking lot all those years ago. He asked if I would come to their temple and speak about Ketan and pray for the peace of his soul at a service planned there. I told the family I would ask Jesus if he felt I should do so. They knew I would do that, and we left pondering the invitation.

The temple in question is near my house, and I know a lot of people who worship there. I have been to many Hindu temples and have been invited to share the gospel at Hindu *satsangs* and *poojas* on a number of occasions, so I did not feel intimidated about that aspect. In fact, for some reason I feel far more intimidated at the thought of preaching in a church full of Christians than in a Hindu temple. However, in this case, I eventually felt it would do more harm than good in the long run, so I declined the invitation. The family was not surprised.

I know that the true worship of Jesus resided within Ketan's family at one time. I know that they were traveling down a discipleship road, but they did not complete the journey. That is what pains me. I wish that Ketan's funeral could have been characterized by a clear testimony of his faith in Jesus, but it was not. I still feel pain over this, and I regret that I could not do more.

Contrast Ketan's story with that of another Gujarati man. Biren (not his real name), who was brought up in the same culture, began attending the various ministries of a church plant that we had started in another town not far from us. What spoke to him was *anubhav*, or experiential knowledge. Everything I seemed to teach Biren and share with him would occur in his life shortly after our conversations, and he would apply what he had heard. We saw good fruit in his life. This opened his heart to the gospel, and he became a follower of Jesus.

When he lay dying of cancer in a hospital, Biren's family sent a group of Hindu fundamentalists and priests to reconvert him to Hinduism. Instead of succumbing to the pressure, Biren did a courageous and admirable thing, the thought of which still sends chills down my spine. He rose up from his hospital bed and told them that he would die with the name of Jesus on his lips. Then he insisted that the Hindu priests leave.

Biren died the next day, and we rejoice that our brother is among the many Hindus who will be worshiping Jesus in eternity.

मार्ग

CHAPTER 3

RELATIONSHIP

SAMBANDH, or relationship, is the beginning of effective witness—to Hindus or to any other group of people. Disciples of Christ
must develop an authentic and sustainable relationship with the people whom they are trying to reach, for it is from this that the entire
movement of growing discipleship toward the lordship of Christ flows.
Relationship is an elementary and essential element of a fruitful gospel
ministry. The Greek word from which we get "gospel" is best understood as "good news." Good news must be delivered by someone who
understands both the message and the people who receive it. Incarnational relationship allows people to learn how to live and communicate
this good news effectively.

Relationship is also fundamental to the ministry of the gospel
among Hindu communities and societies, because Hindu people order their lives, make decisions, and pursue their interests through
webs of meaningful relationships. Hindus will naturally feel more
comfortable if they are introduced to Jesus within the context of
a growing relationship of trust with the disciples of Christ. Any
attempt to influence them to personally accept the gospel, especially through direct evangelistic ministry, without a human being to

process it with will be frustrating at best. Impersonal "mass gospel" messaging may actually do more harm than good, and we must always be careful to do no harm as we spread the gospel.

It is not always easy for Western disciples of Christ to sustain an authentic relationship with Hindus for several reasons. First, there are cultural differences at work. Groups that are culturally diverse do not always have identical or even similar concepts of what constitutes a successful relationship. Concepts and behaviors that create a social environment that is sustainable and authentic for one person or group of people may create a very different situation for someone else. This becomes obvious when we compare and contrast how group and individual values influence one's ability to sustain a successful relationship. For example, many westerners assume that individuals have near-total freedom of association, while many Hindus assume that the family has significant influence over whom the individual family members spend their time with. Of course, like everyone else, Hindus are people, not automatons. Many of them—especially the young men—do things with their friends that their family knows nothing about and would not approve of if they did.

Second, meaningful relationship with Hindus is usually challenging because disciples of Christ may not know how to have authentic, cross-cultural relationships as followers of Christ. Essentially, this means that they may be uncertain how to translate their experience of the lordship of Christ into the relationship in a way that satisfies them and does not alienate their Hindu friends. This is a skill that must be learned. It will require effort, study, and focus. The disciple of Christ will have to grow in knowledge and experience. However, most disciples of Christ do not value these kinds of relationships enough to work at them. Consequently, the vast majority of Hindu people have never experienced a meaningful relationship with someone who can translate their experience of Jesus into a Hindu context.

Third, Hindus and non-Hindus simply live so differently from day to day that sustaining a relationship with them can feel like it requires training, and nobody likes to live like that. For example,

Hindus and non-Hindus usually have completely different values and conceptions around the area of food and drink. These values are not somewhat different; they are really, really different. Hindus also celebrate a different set of holidays, and they also observe family occasions like weddings and birthdays and funerals differently. So this issue of sustainable, authentic relationship is something that we should approach humbly and patiently. The missional heart of God compels us to adjust to Hindus rather than the other way around.

AUTHENTIC, SUSTAINABLE RELATIONSHIPS

The best way to approach sustaining an authentic relationship with a Hindu family is to remember what Scripture teaches us about the nature of gospel witness. The gospel sends the disciples of Jesus outward to take initiative in adjusting to the Hindu family, to enter their world and try to live within the patterns of relationship that are more natural to them. As Christ's disciples, we must take responsibility to learn how to sustain relationship with Hindus rather than expecting them to culturally and socially struggle to "hang out" with us—and indeed, the vast majority of Hindus will never do so. It is God himself who sustains us in these relationships, so we need to draw on his grace consistently.

An authentic relationship is organic, unforced—one that seems take place naturally. This type of relationship is the very best context in which to share the gospel, because it is not necessarily based on any agenda. Colleagues, clients, customers, neighbors, or classmates are examples of these kinds of relationships. This is a much, much better approach than a contrived friendship that is created by believers solely for the purpose of sharing the gospel.

This emphasis on natural, organic relationships does not mean that believers cannot intentionally seek out social or cultural bridges that connect their lives and the lives of Hindus. In fact, this frequently needs to be done, because Hindus and non-Hindus often have very different patterns of life that preclude their paths naturally crossing. Even if a disciple of Christ has a Hindu neighbor, for example, the disciple frequently has to initiate the beginning of a relationship. The Hindus may be slow to respond and for a while appear cold and uninterested, but they are usually just uncertain and self-conscious. The disciple will need to pray for and patiently seek small opportunities to speak with their Hindu acquaintances, but it must not be a bait-and-switch sales approach.

Applying the "person of peace" teaching Jesus gave his disciples is a very sound way to sustain an authentic relationship between Hindus and disciples of Christ. The teaching is found in Matthew 10 and Luke 10. This phrase, "person of peace," is how Jesus describes people who are open to accepting and even embracing a follower of Jesus. The person of peace understands and accepts that the person whom they have met and are getting to know is associated with Jesus. (This often includes the obvious fact that the disciple of Jesus may be from a Christian family.) In a Hindu context, the person of peace is that Hindu who accepts the person who is a disciple of Jesus.

This means that we do not hide our identity as Christ followers. We learn the art of practicing devotion to Jesus in the open, without fear and without a hidden agenda. When asked about our religion or social identity, we wisely and discreetly reveal ourselves as followers of Jesus—but without public announcement or fanfare, because that will stir up any tensions that may already exist between Christians and non-Christians. Jesus modeled this for us in his ministry. He frequently walked away from public acclaim. He wanted to make disciples, not draw a crowd.

The person of peace not only accepts the disciple of Christ, they go even further and invite them into their network of relationships. This may include family and friends. The person of peace knows that their believing friend will continue to be publicly discreet and wisely devoted to Jesus. Furthermore, because of the influence of the person of peace, the other Hindu people to whom they introduce the disciple of Christ will even accept the words of blessing that the disciple offers in Jesus' name, usually in the form of prayer. Again, the disciple is to be careful, tactful, and sensitive. When we seek to enter into the Hindu world, it is extremely important for us to play by their rules, so to speak.

We must not use the person of peace as a means to achieve some sort of Christian mission. Instead, we must accept the way the Hindus live and join them as far as we possibly can. This is the essential truth Jesus was teaching his disciples when he told them to find a person of peace, live with them, and eat with them. Jesus actually encourages us, as his disciples, to enter into the world of Hindu people as deep as our Hindu friends will take us. We are to further seek to be a blessing in any way we can within the social network of the Hindu people of peace. The only boundary is the lordship of Christ—in other words, we will not apostatize in order to relate to the Hindu people within the social network of the person of peace.

It is obviously very important for us to understand the nature of relationships in Hindu culture. When we intentionally seek to develop these kind of relationships with Hindus, we must do so with a frame of mind that enables us to stay in the relationship long-term. We must also be willing to accept the fact that some Hindus may want to distance themselves from us because they do not appreciate or value the presence of Jesus in our life.

COVENANTAL RELATIONSHIPS

Relationships in Hindu culture are covenantal in nature. By covenantal I simply mean relationship that is based on giving and receiving. What Hindus give and receive is respect and acceptance. Acceptance and respect are formalized, because the formalities imply agreements, or covenants, of privilege and obligation between the parties. These privileges and obligations are fulfilled by following a known set of dharmic formalities. Observing them amounts to nothing less than making relationship covenants with one another. This formal relational life is most strictly followed in the extended family, but the covenantal concept of dharmic obligation and privilege pervades Hindu culture and extends outward to friendships and partnerships as well.

As this formal level of covenantal relationship is followed—or at least, not publicly violated—spontaneous, informal friendship that is based on chemistry or having things in common can thrive. We will find that authentic relationship is more sustainable when we stop assuming intimacy without covenant and instead begin to think about attending functions, celebrating holidays, and arranging our life so that it includes the Hindu dharmic calendar. As this formal level of relationship is sincerely observed, informal relationship that is spontaneous, personalized, and intimate can develop.

The Hindu calendar is filled with holidays, festivals, and rites that are the essence of these dharmic observances, and people, families, or *jatis* interact with them in their own way. Giving the expected gifts, attending the required ceremonies and functions, carrying out the rituals that define the dharmic life of the family or community, and in general behaving in the proper way is how Hindus give and receive acceptance and respect from one another. Hindus often refer to this in English as their "social life."

Perhaps the most significant relational formality that impacts how we can sustain authentic relationship with Hindus is eating together. Hindu people do not eat with everybody, and they certainly do not eat everything. Eating with people implies relationship, and if we are invited to eat with the Hindu family, they are granting us a significant level of acceptance. In particular, if they invite us *to their home* for a meal, it communicates that they are granting us an even deeper level of acceptance. And if they are willing to eat in *our* home, they are indicating that they want to live in covenantal relationship with us. This is not always the case, but it is generally true, so we should understand how meaningful it is to be invited to a Hindu home for a meal.

However, this is not an absolute indicator of acceptance, because many higher caste Hindus will not eat with people even from other Hindu castes, let alone with non-Hindus. Some Hindus believe that this may cause moral pollution in the family. There are situations where a Brahmin Hindu family, for example, may be unable to share food or even drink with people from another community, even though they accept them and do want to have a relationship with them. If this is the case, we can allow the Hindus to determine how a relationship with them can be authentic and sustainable, especially if the Hindus share their lives with us in other significant ways. As disciples of Christ, we must become relationally wise and meet Hindus on their own ground.

RELATIONSHIP DEVELOPMENT

The Hindu family will assign to us an identity that is based on how they perceive us. Sometimes this perception will take the form of a nickname. I have been called Trichumdas, meaning "servant of God," several times by Hindu families, and I know of others who have been given different nicknames as well. We cannot stop this, so instead we should try to influence how we are perceived. This means that we must first have an idea of how we *want* to be perceived by the family or group in question, and then do things that will create the desired perception. Of course, our lives must truly match the way we want to be perceived—otherwise we are living hypocritically.

Not only is it crucial for us to have a clear vision of how we want to be perceived, but this needs to be contextualized as much as possible toward Hindu values. For example, a young married man wants to be perceived by a Hindu family as frugal and hard-working, a man who is supporting his parents and children. He does not have time to hang out and "relate" all of the time, but he will make time to meet with people and help someone in need because he values relationships and *seva* (service). A young married woman wants to be perceived as hospitable and welcoming, lovingly serving her children and her husband's parents. A young unmarried woman wants to be perceived as absolutely chaste, focused on her studies, respectful of her parents (and grandparents), yet joyful and fun-loving. Single young men also want to be perceived as chaste and obedient to their parents, as well as preparing for a good job by doing well in college. People with grown children want to be perceived as wise and temperate, spending more time in prayer and study. Of course no one is perfect, but we need to be aware of such perceptions and ask the Lord to lead us into a way of life that is characterized by fruitful work, respect, and service to others.

A relational ministry entails a significant temptation that believers must avoid. This temptation is to "use" the relationship as a platform for the gospel. Disciples often do this because they believe that Hindus will not want to be in an authentic relationship with a devoted follower of Christ. The typical approach is to avoid any sort of witness about one's relationship with Christ, or even any outward display of devotion to Jesus, until after the relationship with the Hindu family is on firmer footing. Then, as the relationship grows toward what the Hindu family believes to be friendship, the believers slowly reveal their faith and/or introduce the gospel, hoping that the affection that exists between them and the Hindu family will carry over into affection for Jesus.

However, if the disciples have contrived a friendship with a hidden agenda of simply sharing the gospel but then discover that the Hindu people are not interested, they have to either break the relationship and leave their Hindu friends or be stuck spending their time with people who have no interest in the Lord. Thus, the disciples have trapped themselves. Even worse, this approach to relational ministry spoils the attitude of Hindu families toward Christ. People who have agenda-driven relationships will always face this situation. There is a better way.

Disciples of Christ, be they from a Hindu or a Christian background, need to be appropriately and naturally open about their devotion to Jesus whenever the conversation or situation leads to that. In this way they free themselves from any agenda or relationship/ministry trap, because they have made the Hindu family aware—as soon as it is natural to do so—that a relationship with them will be a relationship with a person who loves Jesus with their entire being and who loves their neighbor as themselves.

Believers should not hesitate to naturally and winsomely include their devotion to Jesus within the atmosphere of the relationship as soon as possible, avoiding any attempt to point their faith toward the Hindu family. It should be done in a subtle manner, which the Hindu family will completely understand and appreciate. It should not be forced or canned. There is no rush; if a natural way to indicate your devotion to Jesus does not occur for six months, then wait. This is not an attempt to witness or share the gospel. It is a move toward authenticity and away from manipulation, an indirect way of letting the Hindu family know that the believer is religious or spiritual.

A natural, experiential witness is part of how one develops an authentic and sustainable relationship. Open and sincere spirituality without any trace of coercion is a very desirable perception—one that we as believers actually want the Hindu family to have of us, because many Hindus respect people of faith who are genuinely conscious of God. For example, Hindu people may welcome you to the neighborhood or the workplace, and you might simply say something like "We thank the Lord Jesus for our new house," or "We prayed to our Lord Jesus for this new job and he provided for us." You simply tell the Hindu family what happened from your perspective as a Christ follower. You relate stories of how you experience life with Jesus as your Lord. Do not wear people out with an endless narrative, and avoid the "agenda" trap, but do share poignant stories about your experience with Jesus. Hindu families who are conscious of God or in whom the Holy Spirit is already working will respond well to this.

This natural yet open approach to relationship and witness is also the way to give Hindu people a chance to gently and respectfully move away from the relationship if they have no interest in your life as a follower of Jesus. They will realize that they have been given an opportunity to keep the relationship coolly polite and at surface level. If that does happen, you must graciously allow them to back away from a deepening relationship.

It is much better for the Hindu family to back away than for us to break relationship with those who are not open to Christ and with whom we have initiated friendship. If they have backed away, we can then pray for them in private and stay in touch with them in a formal way, all while preserving a cordial friendliness. The sovereign and mysterious timing of God may change the situation at a later time, when he has done his secret work within the Hindu family and begins to draw them to Jesus.

An occupational therapist I know has a patient who is a North Indian Hindu. This therapist is an enthusiastic and devoted follower of Christ. Throughout the interaction that she has with this patient, she mentions faith in God, the grace of God, and her dependence on Jesus' help in her work. She does this naturally and winsomely, and the Hindu man is very impressed with her spirituality, professionalism, and excellence in her practice. She is in an authentic relationship with her patient that is sustainable whether or not he is open to inquiring more about Jesus. In addition to her witness, the therapist often prays privately for the Hindu man to experience the love and grace of Jesus Christ.

Another believer we know, who was in the legal profession and now administrates a college department, has been developing a deepening friendship with a woman from a higher caste Hindu family from northern India. This believer's faith in Christ has always been clear and is a natural part of her conversation. The Hindu woman's family appreciates her spirituality and respects her and her family greatly. These two women share a mutual love for arts and crafts, and they often shop and work on projects together. The relationship has become so close that the Hindu family even gives her the keys to their house whenever they travel to India so she can collect their mail and watch their property. What's more, they have also called upon this believer to give them counsel and pray for them during times of family crisis. Such closeness is rare, and it proves that relationship is everything.

मार्ग

CHAPTER 4

EXPERIENCING
JESUS CHRIST

MANY DISCIPLES of Jesus who live in authentic, sustainable relationship with Hindu people and families also try to faithfully share the gospel with their friends. They do this because they cannot really love someone without sharing the gospel with them. These disciples usually appreciate that living the gospel and sharing the gospel go hand in hand: they realize that the transparent quality of their way of life as followers of Jesus in relationship with Hindu people is the gospel in deed, and they now want to share the gospel in word as well. These kinds of disciples inspire me more than I can put into words.

Such people usually believe that verbal gospel witness that is given with patience, love, and clarity within the context of authentic, sustainable relationship will be fruitful over time. In fact, they may have experienced this truth in ministry with other people in the context of an attractional church, so they are confident of similar results in their attempts to share the love of Christ with Hindus. Again, this is done with relatively pure motives, to bless the Hindu people in whom they are emotionally invested rather than as crass evangelistic number-counting. However, these believers may eventually begin to experience anxiety instead of assurance, because no matter how long and how well they explain the gospel, watering it with prayer and a life that models what they say, their Hindu friends just don't seem to understand. They seem either uninterested or even opposed to the claims of Jesus. This can be very unsettling for the disciple, and unless one knows how to deal with it, it may even lead to a rather serious crisis of confidence in one's call as a witness—perhaps even of faith itself.

Thankfully, Jesus himself had a similar experience, and he shows us how to handle it. He was the greatest communicator who has ever lived. Nobody lived and explained the gospel like him, for he *is* the gospel! Jesus' reaction to this type of situation speaks directly to those of us who love Hindu people.

THE APOLOGETICS OF JESUS

Jesus' disciples lived in an intimate relationship with him for three years. Andrew and Peter had been with him from the very beginning; Andrew had been present at the baptism of Jesus and witnessed the Holy Spirit falling on him. James, John, Phillip, and Nathanael were also very quickly recruited as disciples. Eventually there were around 120 people who formed a community of Jesus' disciples. He was transparent with them, especially with the inner circle of the twelve apostles, holding back nothing about his true identity and the nature of his mission on earth. He had taught them about the kingdom of God in ways that were reserved only for them—a clear explanation that went beyond parables.

As the cross and resurrection drew near, Jesus told his disciples about his departure and his sure return. "Don't fear," he says in John 14. "You know the way to where I am going." The disciples look at each other imploringly, hoping that one of them will say something. Philip finally confesses that they don't really know the way to the Father's house. He also says they want to see the Father too.

Jesus has fully disclosed himself to the disciples over the last three years, and yet they cannot quite understand—or maybe they will not fully believe what he is saying. Jesus, the greatest gospel preacher of all time, can't seem to get through to his disciples! So he offers them evidence to support his teaching. His apologetic is an appeal to recall what they have experienced with him all this while:

> Don't you know me, Philip, even after I have been among you such a long time? Anyone who has seen me has seen the Father. . . . Believe me when I say that I am in the Father and the Father is in me, or at least believe on the evidence of the miracles themselves. I tell you the truth, anyone who has faith in me will do what I have been doing. He will do even greater things than these because I am going to the Father. And I will do whatever you ask in my name so that the Son may bring glory to the Father. You may ask me for anything in my name, and I will do it. (John 14:9–14)

"Believe my words on the basis of my deeds" was how Jesus appealed to his faithless and confused disciples. He meant that his unprecedented deeds and his extraordinary words possessed the same quality of benevolent power, so his actions could provide an apologetic for his words as nothing else could.

The gospel of Jesus Christ is more than words. It is also deeds that, when combined with the verbal message of the good news, provide people with the full, final, and definitive experience of God. This experience is the evidence that people need in order to believe. In fact, the record of his deeds as narrated in the four Gospels is the way people experienced the gospel of Jesus.

Jesus performed many miracles throughout his earthly ministry. He healed the sick, delivered the oppressed from the powers of darkness, and created huge amounts of food to feed thousands of hungry people at a time. He even raised the dead back to life. These miracles were astonishing acts of heavenly power bursting into the physical realm. They reveal Jesus' love for people, and they prove the truth of his claim to be God in flesh. However, Jesus did not use these unprecedented demonstrations of his power as a means to building a following. He frequently withdrew from the crowds, distancing himself from their acclaim and their desire to use him for their own ends. He did this to show us the danger of the ego and the willingness of human beings to use others—or even to be used by others—in order to be popular and publicly powerful. His deeds were about truth motivated by love.

Jesus also did things that were not overtly miraculous yet were just as touched by heaven as were his obvious miracles. For example, he made friends with ordinary people, and they all seemed to like him, even though he was absolutely holy. Ordinary people always have relational problems, which makes the relationships that the Son of God had with them all the more amazing. He even went so far as to interact with prostitutes and unfaithful spouses and crooked tax men. Jesus understood these people and truly cared about them, in spite of—or maybe because of—their undeniable moral and ethical problems. He also played with children and encouraged their stressed parents. Nobody ever did these kinds of things, so nobody—including his disciples—expected *Jesus* to do them either. But one of Jesus' defining characteristics is that he frequently does what is unexpected.

Remarkably, Jesus even went so far as to expose the utter hypocrisy and cultural bigotry of the religious leaders who oppressed ordinary people. Ordinary people would have been nervously thrilled by this, and they were naturally drawn to Jesus. Jesus did many wonderful things, and he appealed to these experiences of his love as evidence of the verbalized truth of his gospel.

But Jesus went still further with Philip and the other disciples: he told them that they would be able to do the same things he had done! They would be able to perform miracles. They would have unexpected and unusual skill in building relationships with normally sinful people—and some *abnormally* sinful people and imperfect human communities. The disciples would even be able to speak truth to help set people free from hypocritical religious powers, even though they were not powerful people themselves.

In John 14 Jesus is telling his disciples that they will be able to do what he did in order to help people experience him even after he has returned to the Father's house. This will be possible by asking Jesus to continue doing the things they have seen him do among them—but now he will do these things through the disciples, who can simply pray in his name. The Holy Spirit, who mediates the presence of Jesus within his disciples, is the one who makes this a reality. Jesus promised this because the apostles—and all who have followed Jesus since—would also need to point to their gospel of deeds to verify the claims of their gospel of words, just as Jesus did, so people might experience God fully, finally, and definitively.

Applying this teaching to a Hindu context can change everything. Disciples who live in authentic relationship with Hindus, but who are filled with anxiety and frustration because they cannot seem to help their friends personalize the gospel, may consider refraining from verbally sharing the gospel. Instead, they can *do* the gospel, as Jesus did, and build a body of evidence that they can point to as an apologetic for the truth of their words. This will bring the Hindu people into the experience of Jesus Christ.

HINDU DHARMA AND EXPERIENCING GOD

Gospel witness to Hindus is a profoundly experiential thing. It is something that *happens* to us—both to the disciples of Jesus who are bearing witness and to the Hindus who are receiving that witness. It happens to us because Jesus is doing it, within us and through us. Experience is a critical part of gospel witness, because it is at the center of a Hindu worldview about truth and religion and God. They want and even *need* to experience Jesus. Furthermore, they will seek to experience him on their own terms, in ways that feel most natural and trustworthy to them. Indeed, *all* human beings approach God in their own way; we cannot help doing so because we are who we are. The fact that God welcomes us however we come to him is a wonder.

In his book *The Hindu View of Life*, the legendary Hindu scholar and first Vice President of Independent India, Dr. Sarvepalli Radhakrishnan, explains the relationship between reasoning and intuition, and the role of experience in grasping truth about God: "Religion . . . is a kind of life or experience. It is insight into the nature of reality or experience of reality. This experience is not an emotional thrill, or a subjective fancy, but is the response of the whole personality" (1927, 13). He further emphasizes the central role of intuitive experience about religion: "Religious experience is of a self-certifying nature. It carries its own credentials" (ibid.).

Radhakrishnan links this self-certifying, intuitive experience to reason; but he uses reason to clarify the experience rather than using experience to complement or illuminate reason. The experience stands until reason catches up:

> In order to be able to say that religious experience reveals reality, in order to be able to translate religious certitude into logical certainty, we are obliged to give an intellectual account of the experience. The chief sacred scriptures of the Hindus, the Vedas, register the intuitions of the perfected souls. They are not so much dogmatic dicta as transcripts from life. . . . The truths in the Vedas can be re-experienced in compliance with ascertained conditions. (1927, 14-15)

Hindu people may look for truth in the sense of a reality that someone has intuitively experienced, and which they can explain and demonstrate how to reproduce. Truth is found within the reasonable narration of the experience, and the proof of the legitimacy of the narrative is that the experience can be reproduced in the real world.

What is the context in which Hindus seek to experience reality? It is dharma. Hindus seek to experience reality that makes a positive difference in the totality of their lives according to Hindu dharma. We must reiterate Bharati's point about the nature of Hinduism: "The most basic point to grasp is that Hinduism is not a religion like other religions but a dharma. . . . So for an average person, dharma is a comprehensive word which includes spiritual, moral, social and even secular values" (2005, 21).

Bharati quotes Benjamin Khan, who further points out that intuitive experience of truth that makes a difference in someone's life will take place in harmony with life in their larger society: "For to create mental and spiritual fellowship among men is the aim of dharma. So the term dharma is a very extensive term and includes all that activity that a man, if he has to live fittingly, is required to contribute under the fixed order of things; it is activity conforming to the norm of the universe which is good and should not be altered" (Khan 1983, 34).

All of this helps us establish a foundational philosophy for experiential gospel witness to Hindus. We are free to apply the insights of Radhakrishnan, Bharati, and Khan because of what Jesus said about an experiential apologetic based on deeds in the Gospel of John.

We can learn at least two things from the material quoted above. First, it is imperative that we learn to conceive of Christianity as the experience of the presence of Jesus within the lives of Hindu people. Wherever and however people experience the presence of Jesus is where his kingdom has come. The Gospel narratives reveal that to experience the presence of Jesus is to be loved by him in a way that is often referred to as blessing: he demonstrates his love by his deeds. In other words, Jesus will reveal himself to Hindu people by blessing them in a manner that they can receive, according to their dharma.

Because their dharma teaches them to live within a highly networked culture of relationships, the presence of Jesus will be experienced by Hindus in such a way that the individual, their family, their community, and potentially even the entire society is blessed. Helping people experience Jesus with a view to their family or larger society is entirely appropriate, because the examples that Jesus left of dealing with people were of blessing, provision, and deliverance rather than of chaos and conflict.

The second thing we learn is that Hindus want to experience Jesus in a way that is intuitive, reasonably explainable, and reproducible. The intuitive experience of Jesus is something that Hindus perceive as righteous and peaceful. They sense the presence of Jesus in the loving deeds that they are experiencing from his disciples. This means that a highly programmatic ministry will not be effective (or even welcome) unless the programs serve to position people together so that they intuitively sense the presence of Jesus among them.

Reasonably explainable experience means that the deeds can be clearly traced as originating with God, who has come to them in Jesus' name, and is not a product of the efforts of people. For example, the Hindu people can point to a prayer ceremony when a certain need was presented to God in Jesus' name—a prayer for healing or deliverance, for example, or a portion of Scripture that shed light on an intractable problem and was the beginning of good news. Verbalizing the gospel message becomes the explanation of how and why we are experiencing Jesus in such a positive way. Stories, examples, and nuggets of truth that sticks are preferable to Christian theology at this point.

Reproducible experience is not formal ritual but something that fits into the Hindu way of life. It is accessible, and Hindus can share it with their family and friends. In fact, this is exactly what Jesus said when he pointed to his deeds as the evidence of the truth of his words, and when he promised his disciples that they would be able to offer the same experience to others through their loving deeds.

The Sanskrit word for this experience is *anubhav*. Anubhav takes place within the soul. It is not the dubious faith of feelings or something that is grasped in a limited way by the senses. Nor can it be reduced to cold rationality, nor taken apart and proven by evidentiary trial, nor weighed by the logical rules of rhetoric. Anubhav is the way God communicates or reveals himself deeply within people.

It is the difference between studying the menu and eating the meal, between planning a trip to the beach and actually walking on the beach. It is a sure experience of hope that the kingdom of heaven can come to earth.

For Hindus, this anubhav is an introductory experience of the benevolent power of Jesus Christ, who surprises them by revealing Himself to them. He enters their world, demonstrating His love and grace. Anubhav may be dramatically powerful, such as the physical miracles performed by Jesus, but it is not strictly a power encounter. It may also be the superb social and relational character that Hindus see in a disciple of Christ who is supporting them in trying or complex circumstances. It may be a startling question that a child asks an adult about the absurdity of biological inequality between groups of people, which unmasks the dark heart of human prejudice. It may be a heartfelt gesture of sincere respect for elders, which pierces the heart of a Hindu family who did not expect to be treated so graciously.

Anubhav can also be a flash of intuitive realization close on the heels of an event that is orchestrated by God, a visible and dramatic answer to a prayer offered to God in Jesus' name, a dream or vision, or an experience of worshipping Jesus in a Hindu manner. It may even simply be peace (*shanti*) in the heart of the Hindu family that "surpasses understanding." Ultimately, the power of anubhav is that it speaks to the Hindu people in a way that awakens their hearts to the reality of Jesus. When experienced consistently and authentically, anubhav gives them assurance about the truth of the gospel.

Anubhav often starts for Hindus when they become convinced that the presence of Jesus is manifested in the lives of his followers. This happens when the disciples have learned not only how to experience Jesus but also how to translate that experience to Hindu people.

Ask yourself this question: How do I experience Jesus? Answering it may require that you adjust your thinking about your relationship with God away from right believing and right doing within an extracted Christian community, and instead direct it toward *experiencing Jesus in everyday life*. Once you have done this, ask yourself a second question: How do I translate this experience into words and practice that Hindu people can intuitively understand, access, and share with others?

Disciples who know how to translate their experience of Jesus into stories that Hindus can access will find it easier to develop a deeper level of trust in their relationship. Their Hindu friends may share a concern or a need, or even an aspiration that they have in their lives with the believers. They may even share that they want to experience Jesus as well. When this happens, the disciple should listen quietly and respectfully, aware that they are being entrusted with a great treasure.

After the disciple is sure that they understand everything clearly, they can assure the family that they will pray to God in Jesus' name about this issue. It may be best to pray for the need privately, or perhaps even arrange a time when they meet with the Hindu family and have a formal prayer ceremony, performed in a Hindu-friendly way. This may include bathing before people gather for the ceremony, sitting on the floor around a small table with burning incense and little candles, and ringing a bell before beginning.

It is best not to push for this, however. Just remain patient and humble and allow the Holy Spirit to show you how to proceed. As you pray, your Hindu friends are in the perfect position to experience the benevolent power of Jesus. Jesus can provide jobs and places to live. He can guide people who are confused about their lives, restore broken families, and heal minds and bodies. When believers and Hindus who are living in authentic relationship share these types of experiences with Jesus, many barriers between them and Jesus can be broken down.

STORIES OF ANUBHAV

Shalini (not her real name) was about sixty when she began attending our ESL classes. She was a charming and friendly person, though it eventually became clear that her quick smile was hiding deep inner pain. One day, after a session in which we had shared our issues and sought prayer in Jesus' name, Shalini told us how frightened and worried she was about her grandchildren. They had grown up in an eastern city in the US and were not always on the same page as her, culturally or morally. Although we had not had this same experience, we could pray for Shalini with insight, because we had lost count of the number of times we had heard this prayer request from other immigrants. Next week she came back and told us the following story.

That week Shalini had been doing *aarti* in her home, just as she had done hundreds of times before. (*Aarti* is a special time of worshiping Hindu deities.) While she waved the small burning wick in the stainless steel plate and prayed, a shining figure dressed in white appeared before her, right there among the idols and pictures and garlands and incense. The person identified himself to her as Jesus. He said that he had heard the prayers she had offered to God in his name for her family. He assured her that all would be well, and then vanished. Shalini wept with joy and awe as she told us this story, and we rejoiced with her.

After this landmark event, we celebrated in Shalini's home with *satsangs*. (*Satsang* is a pan-Indian term meaning "gathering of truth.") We would sing devotional songs called Jesus *bhajans* and have an opportunity to share the gospel with her family and friends. This is an example of anubhav.

Another story is that of Prakash and Jaya (not their real names). The couple had recently moved and misplaced Jaya's gold wedding bangles. They searched their apartment high and low but couldn't find the lost treasure. This was terribly upsetting, and a sense of foreboding about bad luck settled on them. A disciple of Christ who happened to be their friend assured them that he would pray about this situation. The very next day they found the bangles and gave glory to Jesus—right in front of their family! This is also anubhav.

One of the more powerful examples of anubhav is how disciples of Jesus handle adversity and loss. Peace in the midst of trouble is an incredibly powerful anubhav experience for Hindus. A young couple I know had decided to convert to Christianity. They had made the decision to leave self-identification in their birth community and declare Christian identity through church baptism. This was especially complex because the wife was Muslim and the husband was Hindu. They thought conversion would clarify many things in their troubled world, but it had the opposite effect: their families became even more frustrated with them, and then the man lost his job. Since he was in the jewelry business, we talked with them about how trials are more valuable than gold. They decided to persevere and prayed about every issue in their lives. We prayerfully walked with them through this time, and God faithfully guided and provided for them. In the end, their family became completely accepting of their new way of life in Christ. This is anubhav.

A man I'll call Sanjay was also attending our ESL classes. He never missed a session, and I really enjoyed chatting with him and his wife. They were cultured people with attractive personalities, an excellent living example of the wise, temperate, spiritual ideal that Hindus value. One day Sanjay told me that he had begun to notice how every new word or phrase he learned in our class was used in his workplace, just as we said it would be. He saw this as anubhav, an experience of Jesus Christ blessing him because of our love for him, and he died a disciple of Jesus.

Another man came to believe that Jesus' presence was in our lives, and since we were outside the Hindu community he felt safe with us. One summer his son fell very ill and was hospitalized. Our friend blamed himself for this. He had heard from us and from Christians in India that Jesus was the God who would forgive sin. Anubhav was working in his mind. One day he arranged to meet me and confessed horrific sins he had committed in India, hoping I would bring him to Jesus so he could escape what he saw as God's wrath. Many Hindus believe that their bad karma is worked out in the lives of their children. I listened carefully to his confession and prayed with him. I urged him to join me in the process of seeking Jesus for forgiveness and a new life. This brother truly sought the Lord, but his wife hated us and destroyed any further attempt at witness.

A transformed life is a powerful anubhav for Hindus. We know of a young man from the global Hindu diaspora who had fallen into a life of substance abuse. However, his conversion to Christianity, which involved water baptism in a church and referring to himself as a Christian, completely changed his life from hatred to blessing. This led his family to become Christ *bhaktas*, followers of Jesus who retain a Hindu identity.

Experiencing Jesus through answered prayer is another powerful form of anubhav. A man we know came from an upper caste family that was filled with chaos and self-destructive tendencies. He had experienced provision in Jesus' name, which, through a series of events, helped him rescue his sisters from disastrous arranged marriages. This man grew rapidly in his faith, and was once even invited to share the gospel in a leading Hindu temple in India! His father eventually accepted his Christ bhakti—devotion to Christ— and one of his sisters became a Christ bhakta herself.

DEVOTION OR CONVERSION

After a Hindu family has had an introductory anubhav, they may become very open to welcoming Jesus further into their lives. This is a crucial moment or period of time for Hindus on their journey to Christ, so the believers must allow them to respond to Jesus from the heart. In other words, they must allow the Hindus to respond to Jesus *as Hindus*, so that their faith will be sincere and real.

Hindus usually don't respond positively to Jesus or "get saved" like nominal, unregenerate Christians. They respond positively to Jesus like *Hindus*, through devotion that motivates them to seek to worship him. This worship will deepen the anubhav that the Hindus have already had and make Jesus even more attractive, convincing them that they can approach Jesus and relate to him from an undivided heart.

Often, however, our fears about syncretism, doctrine, and "the way we were raised" prevent us from understanding this process.

We assume that all people receive Christ in much the same way, so we ask Hindus if they are willing to accept Christ as their Savior. "I already accept Jesus," they think, and say yes. At this point we disciples, anxious to be faithful to the gospel, press the Hindus to understand and accept that Jesus must be their only God.

Hindus may not understand what accepting Christ really means to the disciple. But if they get the sense that the anubhav comes at the cost of being pressured to become Christians, we are likely to lose any ability to help them further understand who Jesus really is and what he would like to fully accomplish in their lives. We may deeply offend them and never even know it—they might gradually distance themselves from us because they think we are insisting that they convert to Christianity.

A ministry philosophy that emphasizes conversion as the basis of devotion will almost always have this effect. This is not what is meant by the offense of the gospel. It is just inappropriate ministry practice.

Believers may want to push for conversion, but it is much better to empower *devotion*. Hindus refer to this as bhakti. Bhakti means devotion, and that devotion can certainly be focused on Jesus, regardless of whether the bhakta has said the Sinner's Prayer. Devotion through worship is the heartbeat of how Hindus respond to God after a positive initiatory experience of Jesus. The revolution for believers is not only to accept this but to actually empower Hindus to worship Jesus, even if they have not yet confessed the lordship of Christ. Experience that is followed by worship is the very best way to reproduce the experience of truth, according to Dr. Radhakrishnan—and more importantly, according to Jesus in John 14.

Jesus-focused bhakti motivates the Hindu family to truly consider the feasibility of life as disciples who are devoted to Jesus. As they wrestle with the implications of this life-changing and unexpected revelation, they will naturally need to consider how other Hindu people will respond to their new devotion. Will their family and friends continue to accept them, or will society reject them?

This is often the point where everything breaks down, but it does not have to be the end. There is an alternative.

This other possibility is for the Hindu family to consider that their devotion to Jesus as Hindus, not as converts to Christianity, could be acceptable—even attractive and inviting—to their family and friends. They might come to believe that the people they love could also experience Jesus, that they too could pray to him, worship him, learn about him, and witness to others about him.

APPROACHING WORSHIP

When disciples of Christ have an authentic, sustainable relationship with Hindu people who are experiencing Jesus, they can introduce the family to the possibility of worship. It will probably not occur to the Hindus to approach the believers (but if it does—marvelous!).

The believers can invite the Hindu family to participate in worship with them in whatever way the believers do so. This could include attending a worship service at a church, but this should be handled cautiously. The believers must take great care to avoid giving any sense that they are trying to convert the Hindus into Christians. The culture of the church should also be considered. If its members are not open minded or are unable to lovingly receive non-Christians into their service, then do not take Hindus there. There are certainly Hindu people who will respond well to a suggestion to attend a Christian worship service, but many more will not value it.

It is best to have a time of worship in your natural surroundings, like your home. If you worship Jesus from time to time, invite your Hindu friends to come and experience this worship with you. Perhaps you could plan a special time of worship, simple but authentic and heartfelt, thanking Jesus for what he has done for the Hindu family. If the Hindu family agrees, ask them to help you arrange a way to worship and thank Jesus. They may respond nervously, having no idea how to worship Jesus, and ask you to do it.

The better way, however, is to begin a dialogue with them about worship; draw bhakti out of their heart. Ask them how worship is done in their world. They may be unsure how to respond and ask you a lot of questions. Answer their questions about worship in a straightforward way, naturally using the Bible when necessary— but do not take over, because a wonderful thing is happening. The Hindu family is willingly trying to align themselves with Jesus in a meaningful way.

The best situation by far is when the elders in the family are leading the dialogue and trying to use their own worship forms to worship Jesus. They may want to sing to him, thank him in some sort of ceremony, speak his name with reverence, or pray to him again with love and faith. They may want to use candles and incense. To be perfectly candid, I know many Hindus who want to incorporate a picture of Jesus to use during a worship service. But this is not idolatry; it is more like Christian use of symbols or icons. They may want to do this in a worship party where they implement the method of worship that has been discovered and then eat together. This is very common.

One unique element of bhakti that we have already mentioned briefly is *bhajan,* a style of music that characterizes much of the Hindu worship tradition. *Bhajan* also refers to a song in this style, and the verb form of *bhajan* means "to worship." Hindu people know how to sing bhajans and will teach you. Since they are still culturally connected to India, they may want to worship Jesus in a more Indian bhajan style, sitting on the floor and using Indian musical instruments. They may need to write their own bhajans about Jesus. The disciples of Christ may ask their Hindu friends to do that. That would be simply incredible! The Christian communities of India all have bhajan-style music in their worship traditions that can be used by Hindus. These are often very rich and meaningful songs, written and sung in bhajan format. It is perfectly fine to worship Jesus in a bhajan style.

SYNCRETISM AND EXCLUSIVITY

The disciples of Christ have to make a decision to trust the instincts of the Hindu family and accept their ways of worship. The only issue for the believers would be if the worship being discussed included the worship of other deities along with Jesus. This is very delicate and can be difficult. I personally find it disheartening when the worship of Jesus is not distinguished from the worship of deities whom I strongly believe are not representative of the true and living God, but there is also a wonderful opportunity here.

How the believers respond to this will be a living example of how Hindus who are the only disciples of Jesus within their families can respond to difficult situations when other deities are being worshipped. At that point, the believers should gently inform the Hindu family that when the worship of other deities takes place, they will not participate. The believers will not leave, but they will politely not participate in the worship of any other gods or goddesses because the believers have an exclusive relationship with Jesus. The Hindu family will understand this type of relationship and will not pressure the disciples of Christ.

Your Hindu friends might inquire if they too should only worship Jesus. You should not tell them what to do, but instead clearly explain what an exclusive relationship with Jesus is all about. The best way to explain your exclusive relationship with Jesus is to use examples from the life and culture of Hindu families. Their lives are filled with examples of the one among the many, and we can use those daily life examples to explain why we are exclusively devoted to Jesus. This approach is exactly how Jesus taught people deeper truth; he used simple examples from their way of life.

A good example emerges from the Hindu family. There are many different men in a Hindu family, and each one has a title depending on who he is related to. A paternal uncle, a maternal uncle, or an uncle by marriage all are a part of our lives, but only one man—my father—gives me life, so I honor him in a unique and special way.

Likewise, there are many gods and goddesses in the world, but only Jesus has given me eternal life, so I honor and serve him.

Another powerful example of the one among the many that speaks to Hindus is in marriage. There are many women in the world, but I am in an intimate love relationship with just one woman: my wife. There are many deities in the world, but I am lovingly devoted to Jesus alone.

Both of these examples communicate a "Hindu friendly" exclusivity that almost always satisfies the questions that people may have. When this type of discussion happens while Hindus who have experienced Jesus are attempting to worship him, it is a powerful gospel testimony indeed.

CONCLUSION

Moving away from conversion as the basis for devotion, to devotion as the means and end of how Hindus respond positively to Jesus, can bring us great relief from the often self-imposed guilt that we feel about witness. A much healthier ministry philosophy is that of empowering Hindus to grow as devotees of Jesus; their devotion and worship of Jesus reveal their faith in Jesus. It is an extremely powerful witness for believers to be living in authentic, sustainable relationship with a Hindu family that is experiencing Jesus. The believers now should begin to look for opportunities to build on this foundation and bring the family the gospel message about the death and resurrection of Jesus Christ.

मार्ग

CHAPTER 5

CLARIFYING THE EXPERIENCE:

TEACHING THE GOSPEL OF JESUS CHRIST

HINDUS WHO ARE living in authentic relationship with Christ's disciples, and who are experiencing the gospel of Jesus through answered prayer and worship, must have that experience clarified. This happens as the disciples carefully use Scripture to explain the core of the gospel and attribute it as the reason for this unexpected experience of Jesus' benevolent and powerful presence.

Hindus generally do not need an apologetic that demonstrates the reliability of Scripture, because they are usually open and respectful toward any form of religious scripture, including the Bible. Obviously they will not automatically assume the Bible to be ultimate, authoritative truth. They see it as one form of truth, or one version of truth among many. However, since the Bible is the inspired word of God, simply using it often reveals its depth and insight to Hindus, and they often come to love it just by being exposed to it.

This is a significant point to remember, because using the Bible is not always so easy in other contexts. Secular westerners do not simply accept the Bible as truth, and neither do Muslims. There may be cases where highly educated, westernized Hindu people also question the use of Scripture, and in these cases a straightforward dialogue about why we trust and use the Bible might be helpful. Otherwise, if no objections are raised, it is advisable to just use Scripture to teach the gospel.

But this experience, or anubhav, must be clarified, because an experiential gospel witness can contain certain deceptive dangers. The most obvious and common one is the belief that God will give us everything we want and nothing we don't want if we approach him in Jesus' name. This type of magical thinking about our relationship with God is very prevalent in Christian circles. The Hindu version of it is derived from a worldview in which people can get God to do what they ask if they approach him according to a prescribed set of principles and rituals, almost always through the agency of a religious professional like a priest or guru.

This mindset is usually transferred over to experiencing Jesus, so that people think that if they approach God correctly, in the name of Jesus, God will have to do what they ask. If he doesn't do what they expect or desire even though they have followed the rules, Hindus may become confused and anxious. The ominous expectation at that point is the fear that something bad will happen to them or their family, because things have gotten dangerously out of control. This will almost always lead Hindus to withdraw from Jesus, thus never becoming mature disciples.

Clarity about the benevolent power of Jesus Christ helps us move away from "using" Jesus as a way to get what we want. Instead, we place the experience within a growing perspective of surrender to grace and truth rather than falling into the lie of thinking we can control our life by controlling God. The truth about God's grace is that the experience, or anubhav, is a door that God has graciously opened, beckoning us to enter. Entering through the door of anubhav leads to our experiencing the presence of Jesus, who wants to give us a transformative relationship with God. The experience is just the beginning of coming to clarity about our relationship with God.

Anubhav must also be clarified because Hindus may have a lot of questions—and they are all good questions—about why all of this is happening to them. For example, they may not understand why God blesses them in Jesus' name since they are not Christians. They respect Jesus, but they never ever expected him to enter their lives in this way. They may even have anxiety about the implications of the undeniable presence of Jesus, the God of the Christians, coming into their family. It is therefore imperative that we avoid a christianization that is connected to church and conversion, where much of the stress and anxiety are located. Instead, we must focus on Jesus Christ within the context of the people's way of life as Hindus.

We clarify the experience by introducing them to the core of the biblical gospel—namely, the person and work of Jesus Christ. We do so by translating the gospel into their Hindu world. Since only the gospel can explain the unexpected experience of Jesus' benevolent power, we clarify it by teaching the gospel as the answer to why and how it is happening.

BIBLE STUDY IN THE HINDU CONTEXT

There are two ways to conduct a Bible study in the Hindu context. The first is to present the gospel as the full story of Jesus, including the prophecies about the Messiah, his life and deeds and teachings, as well as the events surrounding his passion, including his death, resurrection, and ascension. The other is to see the gospel as a system of ideas and propositions emphasizing man's sinful condition and God's solution in Christ.

These two ways are not opposing ideas but rather complementary parts of a full gospel, so to speak. It is wise, however, to heed the advice of George David, a pioneer missionary in North India:

> Ninety percent of the time when we attempt to communicate the gospel, we preach a formula instead of

narrating the story of Jesus. As Christian communicators, we need to learn the art of narrating the
stories of Jesus in a simple and vivid manner. Our
business as communicators of the gospel is basically
to narrate the stories of Jesus in prose, poetry and in
bhajan form, and to demonstrate through the lives
of the disciples and the communities of practising
disciples. Only then do we communicate the gospel
in ways that are digestible and meaningful to our
Hindu friend. (1998, 77)

Presenting the gospel in order to clarify the experience that
Hindus have had incorporates both approaches, and it contextual-
izes them for Hindu people. The following paragraphs will list the
process step by step.

Begin by reading the narrative of Jesus' arrest, death, and resurrection, but remember that Hindus do not have Christian echoes
in their mind. They most likely do not know about the events surrounding the death and resurrection of Christ, and they will be
unable to understand any teaching about it until they learn what
actually happened. Reading Matthew 27 and 28 and discussing the
story is very powerful indeed. Take all the time that is needed to go
over the events, without feeling the pressure to rush through it. It
is also helpful to go as far back into the Gospel narrative of Christ's
life as the situation requires before discussing the meaning of the
death and resurrection of Christ.

After the Hindu readers have a grasp of the events that are recorded in Matthew 27–28, the meaning of those events must be
explained. Romans 8:31–34 and Philippians 2:5–11 are helpful passages for this, and both should be used so that the fullness of the
gospel becomes clear. These scriptures speak with clarity and power
to Hindu people who are experiencing the benevolent power of Jesus and wondering why or how it is happening. Let us examine how
each passage does this.

Romans 8:31–34

> What, then, shall we say in response to these things? If God is for us, who can be against us? He who did not spare his own Son, but gave him up for us all—how will he not also, along with him, graciously give us all things? Who will bring any charge against those whom God has chosen? It is God who justifies. Who then is the one who condemns? No one. Christ Jesus who died—more than that, who was raised to life—is at the right hand of God and is also interceding for us.

This scripture speaks to the anubhav in at least four ways. First, it addresses the questions of anxiety. When the Hindus wonder why they, as Hindus, are experiencing Jesus, the God of the Christians, verse 31 says, "What then shall we say in response to these things?" It tells them that it is perfectly understandable to be anxious about this issue, but there is no need to be afraid, confused, or angry, because "if God is for us, who can be against us?"

Second, this scripture connects God's goodness and love to his Son, whom he gave up for us. If God loves people enough to give his Son for them, then he will also give us everything else that is good for us: as verse 32 says, "He who did not spare his own Son, but gave him up for us all—how will he not also, along with him, graciously give us all things?" This is why the gospel literally means *good news*.

Third, it is important to explain what it means that God gave his Son for us, and why this results in him blessing us in Jesus' name. The answer begins to emerge by the revelation that God chooses us: we are chosen to receive the benevolent power of God in Jesus' name. At this point we must make sure not to wander about in the age-old bog of sovereignty and free will, which is so much a part of Western theological controversy. Rather, we must simply reveal to our Hindu friends that God has chosen them to be blessed in this way. This always encourages them greatly, and it actually makes sense to them. It also helps them explain why the Christian God is present in their midst to family or friends who may be upset: They didn't seek this out—Jesus sought them out and chose them. God justifies his work in their lives through Jesus, even though they are Hindus, because they have been chosen to be blessed by him. Therefore, as verse 33 says, "Who will bring any charge against those whom God has chosen? It is God who justifies. Who then is the one who condemns? No one."

Fourth, verse 34 tells us that Jesus blesses us because he is seated at the right hand of God, interceding for us. His intercession is benevolent, powerful, and true because of his death and resurrection. In his death, he showed that he is a true guru. Many Hindus believe that true gurus are not really overtaken by the inevitability of death. Instead, they choose to leave the body. This is known as *samadhi*. Jesus knew he was going to die and rise again. His life was not taken from him. He gave his life, taking samadhi, which reveals that he is a true guru. (In this regard, John 10:14–18 also speaks very clearly to Hindus.)

In his resurrection, Jesus broke the power of karma and rebirth, or sin and death, because he returned to life in the same body in which he had died. This is important because it confronts the core concept of karma and reincarnation. The vast majority of Hindus believe that karma attaches itself to the soul, or *atma*. The atma takes a form (or birth) according to the nature of the karma attached to it. If the karma is good, the result is a good life. Bad karma leads to suffering. No karma leads to no further rebirth. In a nutshell, that is the Hindu view of justice.

Jesus lived in such a way that his atma was free from karmic attachments, because he only did what God, whom he called his Father, told him to do. And yet, even though his atma was pure and completely free of all karmic attachments, Jesus took samadhi and then returned to life in the same physical body. His body was changed and is now perfect and beyond corruption and death. This means that he is the Lord of karma, with an authority that is greater than the inevitability of karma. As the Lord of karma, Jesus

returned to the world in his body because he values the transformation of the human body, and of all creation, into a perfect form as
much as he values the release of the human atma.

Jesus is now at the right hand of God, where he intercedes for
us, choosing us and blessing us with the experience of his benevolent power. He does this so we will realize that eternal life at the
right hand of God is in his name. As Romans 8:34 says, "Christ
Jesus who died—more than that, who was raised to life—is at the
right hand of God and is also interceding for us."

Philippians 2:6–11

> [Christ Jesus], being in very nature God, did not
> consider equality with God something to be used
> to his own advantage; rather, he made himself
> nothing by taking the very nature of a servant, be-
> ing made in human likeness. And being found in
> appearance as a man, he humbled himself by be-
> coming obedient to death—even death on a cross!
> Therefore God exalted him to the highest place and
> gave him the name that is above every name, that at
> the name of Jesus every knee should bow, in heaven
> and on earth and under the earth, and every tongue
> acknowledge that Jesus Christ is Lord, to the glory
> of God the Father.

This is another scripture that clarifies and deepens the anubhav. It is often a powerful follow-up to the revelation of the gospel
in Romans 8, because it helps Hindus wrestle with the exclusive
claims of Jesus as Lord.

First, this passage reveals that Jesus existed eternally as God,
God the Son, yet he emptied himself to serve humankind. He did
this by actually becoming a human being. Because Jesus was fully
God and fully human, he was the perfect man, and some Hindus
will immediately conceive of him as *Purushottam*, or perfect man.

The perfect humanity Jesus shows is one of *seva*, or service to God among people: verses 6 and 7 say that Jesus, "being in very nature God, did not consider equality with God something to be used to his own advantage; rather, he made himself nothing by taking the very nature of a servant, being made in human likeness."

Second, Jesus proved that he was Purushottam by showing us what perfect devotion to God and seva in the world looks like. His obedience was so complete that it led him to death on the cross. *How could this have happened?* Hindus may wonder. It is because of sin: sin causes death. All people sin and therefore all people die. Jesus, as Purushottam, never sinned, yet he certainly died. Why was this? It was *our* sin that caused his death. He served us by dying for us! Jesus loved God the Father and us so much that he experienced our sin and our death. As verse 8 says, "Being found in appearance as a man, he humbled himself by becoming obedient to death— even death on a cross!"

Third, because of this, God raised him from the dead and exalted him. His name is now above every name, which means that God blesses people in the name of Jesus because Jesus is Lord of all. Absolutely *everybody* has the opportunity to receive him as their Lord and be free from sin! As the last three verses in this passage declare, "Therefore God exalted him to the highest place and gave him the name that is above every name, that at the name of Jesus every knee should bow, in heaven and on earth and under the earth, and every tongue acknowledge that Jesus Christ is Lord, to the glory of God the Father."

This, then, is a basic Hindu-friendly introduction to the core of the gospel as revealed in the Bible: begin with Matthew 27–28, then go to Romans 8, and then to Philippians 2. Teach it clearly and patiently. But notice, faith is missing. How do we approach faith?

Worship or devotion is what reveals Hindus' faith. When we share Jesus in the Hindu context, we must aim for devotion rather than conversion, because devotion is based on faith. This is what James 2:14–26 means when it talks about the connection between faith and works. Works reveal faith. In a Hindu context, bhakti and seva are two parts of one spiritual whole that reveals the presence of faith.

It is certainly the believer's responsibility to clearly and accurately communicate the gospel, but the believer cannot determine in advance what a positive response to the gospel will look like or how it will manifest itself in the life of the Hindu family. Hindus must remain free to approach faith in Jesus *as Hindus*, so the cross of Christ can impact them at the deepest levels of their lives. As the believers teach the gospel message over time, they adopt a responsive posture: they continue to live in authentic relationship with the family, but gradually add dialogue as the Hindus seek to discover how they can respond to the gospel's claims about Jesus.

There will be two positive responses. Some Hindu families may want to call themselves Christians as they receive Christ. That is fine if it is *their* desire, if the idea originates with them. But for others, surrender to Christ will lead them to become Christ bhaktas—disciples of Jesus who retain a Hindu identity. The heart response to the gospel for everybody is always one of surrender, by which we mean the inner surrender of one's heart and life to become a follower of Christ.

IDENTITY

Well-meaning believers often conceive of evangelism as calling Hindus to make a one-time, full commitment to Jesus. We want Hindus to give up all of India's gods and goddesses, reject belief in reincarnation, and believe exclusively in Jesus. It can be very hard not to do that, in fact—but it is almost always a mistake to take the initiative and confront them with this choice. When disciples tell a Hindu family that they must stop living as Hindus in some way in order to embrace Christ, what Hindus hear is this: "Jesus will not really accept me if I'm Hindu. He only accepts Christians."

That may not be at all what the believers want to communicate, but it is usually how the Hindus interpret this type of exhortation, and it almost always offends them. It sounds condemning of their family and heritage and comes across as uncritically exalting of the believer's family and heritage. It also seems to place the believers in a judgmental position over the Hindus. Christians usually assign a religious and spiritual connotation to "Hindu" and "Christian," whereas Hindus interpret these terms more as designations of culture or community. So the advice that to embrace Jesus they must stop believing or doing something they have believed or done all their lives sounds like a personal rejection. This is not the offense of the gospel. It is merely an inappropriate approach.

Our challenge is to help Hindus develop a faithful and fruitful relationship with Jesus without condemning them along the way. It is far better to speak positively about the fullness of Christ, and the subsequent surrender of our hearts to him, without even mentioning other deities. Instead of putting pressure where it is not necessary, Christ's followers need to journey with Hindus as they grapple with surrender to Jesus, supporting them and helping them find answers to their questions and problems.

SURRENDER

The Sanskrit term *sharanam* means surrender. It is used in a highly devotional context in Hindu culture, describing the person who is utterly abandoned to God, and it is the call of God to the Hindu heart: "Surrender to Jesus."

Traveling with Hindus in authentic relationship through anubhav and bhakti, helping them understand and personalize the gospel and finally arrive at surrender to Jesus, usually takes place within an atmosphere of inner struggle. Hindus may experience self-doubt, identity crisis, family pressure, and even open conflict during this journey. Therefore, believers and Hindus alike need to stay positive and patient, focusing on the person and work of Jesus alone without any other agenda as he leads them all on this perilous road to sharanam—total surrender to Jesus.

Hindus sometimes seem to surrender to Jesus in a series of stages. The stages have to do with a growing trust or faith in Jesus as their exclusive Lord. They begin by praying to Jesus among their original deities. Then they will pray to Jesus as their chief deity. At the next stage Jesus becomes their *Ishta Devata*, their chosen and exclusive Lord, and finally they acknowledge him as the supreme Lord of everybody in the world.

Higher caste Hindus may begin to surrender by accepting Jesus as a god whom they can pray to. This often happens after they have an initiatory anubhav. It helps them develop a love for Jesus, whom they now begin to worship along with all of their other deities. This stage is characterized by syncretistic thinking and worship, but worship of Jesus will speak to them and help them work through this syncretism, because worship deepens and widens their anubhav of Jesus. The anubhav is the foundation upon which to share the gospel, and the gospel is presented as the reason for the anubhav.

The next stage of surrender happens as Hindus plumb the depths of the death and resurrection of Christ. In light of Christ's awesome love and power exhibited in the cross and the empty tomb, and given the way their own lives have been blessed by Jesus, Hindus may gradually find that that they have no further need or desire for other deities. At this point they will personally surrender to Christ and Christ alone: he becomes their Ishta Devata, their chosen God. Let other Hindus pray to whomever they wish, but from this time forward *we* will pray exclusively to Christ, they decide.

The final stage of surrender is when Hindus realize that Jesus is indeed Lord of all. He is not the Western God, nor is he the God of Indian Christians. He is not just *my* Ishta Devata. He is the Lord of all people all over the world.

There is always one critical issue that accompanies this stage of surrender. Hindus will wonder and eventually ask about the eternal destiny of people who have not become devotees of Christ. What is their destiny? Knowing the answer to this question is not as important as knowing *how* to answer it.

Needless to say, great care must be taken to be nonjudgmental and reasonable. The usual Christian debates about the fate of those who have never heard the gospel, or the nature of eternal judgment, will simply not suffice at this point because of one simple but determinative fact: *Hindus aren't Christians.* They do not think in terms of systematic theology, church history and church councils, the Reformation, Purgatory, or such things. This issue is not the litmus test of biblical orthodoxy for them, as it is for many conservative Western Christians. Hindus want to approach this in a reasonable, fair, and practical manner, and they will do so *as Hindus.*

The best way I have found to answer this is to stress that Jesus is the Judge of all people because he has risen from the dead, as the apostle Paul says in his Mars Hill sermon (Acts 17:29–31). When we refer to Jesus as the Judge, we mean much more than that he will dispense punishment to those who do not believe in him. That is a significant misunderstanding of the extent to which he is the Judge. The reality is that Jesus is the only one who is authorized by God to make decisions about the destiny of people, because his death and resurrection positioned him to do that. He has already told us that he alone will determine who goes into the presence of God after death (John 14:6).

Jesus has also told us how he will deal with those who are not his disciples. He will evaluate or judge them based on their works or their deeds. This takes place at the end of time, when all people who have not yet received Christ stand before him as he judges their works, their deeds, and their way of life. What will happen to them will be a result of how Jesus evaluates their life, as we learn from Revelation 20:11–15. This approach is not only biblical, but it also seems satisfactory to Hindu people, who already have a worldview that assumes that all of our deeds have repercussions. Once this is brought out, it is best to simply leave it as it is, respectfully allowing Hindu people the time they need to process this very weighty truth. It is a powerful teaching that will deeply impact any Hindu person who is gradually surrendering to Christ.

So what does all of this look like in overview? As Hindus and believers in Jesus live in an authentic and sustainable relationship, they will have the opportunity to experience Jesus together. That experience is a demonstration of his benevolent power. If the Hindus respond positively to this introductory anubhav, they may be open to begin worshipping Jesus, and this will further add to their anubhav. When this is followed by a step-by-step presentation of the gospel, which is given as the reason for the anubhav, the gospel will deepen and clarify the anubhav.

Over time, as Hindus continue to experience Jesus through worship and prayer within the context of relationship with Christ's disciples, they will begin to apply the implications of the gospel to their experience and gradually surrender to the lordship of Christ. Eventually, the believers realize that a deeper level of discipleship is needed.

CHAPTER 6

INTENTIONAL DISCIPLESHIP

BY NOW YOU and your Hindu friends have come a long way together. You have developed an authentic, sustainable relationship in which you experience the living Lord Jesus in real life, as well as in planned and intentional prayer and worship. This anubhav is changing how the Hindu people conceive of Jesus. They are coming to realize that Jesus is not encapsulated within the beliefs or practices of a human culture, such as Western or even Indian Christianity, and thus he is not lost to them. Instead, they have discovered that Jesus is a living God, and they are processing the startling truth that he is the true and *only* living God who transcends culture to bless mankind. Furthermore, the Hindus are gradually becoming convinced that Jesus is not only real but can actually be a part of their lives, even though they are not from a Christian background.

As a result of this transformative anubhav, your Hindu friends are beginning to be devoted to Jesus along with you. This emerging devotion to Jesus has also motivated them to listen to a fairly detailed presentation of the biblical gospel message, which explains why we can truly experience the benevolent and powerful presence of Jesus today, even though the events of his life recorded in the Bible happened two thousand years ago.

As far as you can tell, your Hindu friends are starting to understand the gospel and are personalizing its truth. It seems that they have joined you on the path of surrender to Jesus as their Savior and Lord. Whether they are still sincerely processing what the gospel means to them, or whether they have actually become gospel-confessing believers, it is now time to travel with them further down the road of devotion to Jesus.

INTENTIONAL DISCIPLESHIP REBOOT

We often conceive of evangelism and discipleship as two separate things. The person who is sharing the gospel actively tries to persuade the other, who passively listens and does little more than observe and evaluate. After the latter trusts in Christ, the older believer begins to disciple the new believer so they learn all that they need to know to become true followers of Jesus. The new believer continues to passively listen and absorb the information, occasionally asking questions. Eventually discipleship, as distinct from evangelism, becomes very collaborative as the new believer joins the Christian community.

This may make perfect sense when the believer who has initiated evangelism, and then conscientiously followed that with discipleship, is culturally and linguistically identical to the new believer and is able to lead them in a truly insider conversation about Jesus. The conversation can be held at a deep level, with little or no cultural confusion. However, we err when we think that this is exclusively a result of the work of the Holy Spirit. It is that, but it is also simply a way that fruitful gospel-sharing ministry between cultural insiders can happen.

Often disciples of Christ mistakenly think that they should conduct gospel ministry to Hindus in the same way—that is, by separating evangelism and discipleship and only very gradually partnering with them in discipleship. But that should not be the case in any cross-cultural disciple making, because the disciple who initiates ministry is a cultural outsider, and they actually need help from the people they are trying to introduce to the gospel to be able to communicate effectively. It is certainly the case with Hindus, and it is the primary reason why relationship is so important. Trust must be developed, because we need them to help us understand what to do and say. They must trust us and we must trust them. This takes place within an authentic, sustainable relationship.

A relational discipleship ministry is a collaboration between Hindus and disciples of Jesus. Because Christians need Hindus in this way, the basis for separating evangelism and discipleship disappears. Christians are in a collaborative ministry with Hindus from the very beginning as they share areas of need and growth and help each other explain the gospel and grow in Christ. Thus Hindus actually help their mentor evangelize and disciple them!

The best example of this is when Hindus inform their mentor about challenging situations and difficult life issues for which they need solutions. In response, the mentor helps them seek out biblical teaching concerning the issue. In this scenario the Hindus help their mentor interpret the biblical teaching and apply it to their lives wisely and practically, and the mentor lets them do so, because they trust the work of the Holy Spirit and humbly accept that the Hindus are fully capable of understanding how to live out biblical teaching in their own lives. This creates missional energy and focus from the get-go. Thus, the Hindus are not passive as the ministry evolves, but they contribute to it much more than the disciples may initially realize.

COVENANTAL RELATIONSHIPS AND DISCIPLESHIP

The most important reality in the life of Hindus is their family. This means that relationship with parents, siblings, and a host of cousins, aunts, and uncles is the stuff of life for them. This highly relational lifestyle also spills over into deep, long-term friendships with people who are not a part of their family. We have seen that these familial relationships are covenantal in nature.

Westerners generally fight this, because they believe supremely in individual freedom. Indian Christians do not fight it since their family arrangements are much the same as those of Hindus. But in either case, whether the mentor is a Westerner or an Indian Christian, the controlling reality of family presents problems to a typical Christian concept of discipleship. The family is usually seen as the reason why the individual Hindu cannot become a disciple. Some will go as far as to suggest (or even insist) that Hindus disregard their family to follow Jesus. Frankly, this is a bad approach to making disciples. Christians all over the world must learn to think deeply and bravely about discipling individuals in the context of family, or even discipling entire families, for God instituted family as a foundational element of his kingdom.

What is the relationship between this family-oriented culture and discipleship to Jesus? Is it possible for Hindus to be disciples of Jesus and still keep covenant with their family, which is the essence of being Hindu? Absolutely! In the Hindu context, covenantal expectations are fulfilled and relationship is maintained by observing interpersonal formality and custom that follows the prescribed way of life. If this is done, Hindu believers in Jesus can remain within their Hindu family. In some families they can even negotiate their level of participation as long as the family knows that they sincerely plan to keep covenant with all of them. The challenge before us, then, is to make disciples whose faith in Jesus *enhances* their ability to keep covenant with their family rather than weakening it.

Historically, and even currently, "conversion" of a Hindu person to Christ has often greatly threatened this covenantal way of life. Sadly, in many instances it has even destroyed it. Discipleship of Hindu people without a commitment to the Hindu family often forces Hindus to choose between maintaining covenantal relationship with their family or subscribing to the Christian culture of those who are discipling them, which usually consists of faithful church attendance and adopting all the Christian formalities, including holidays, eating together, and sacraments. It puts an enormous pressure on the Hindus to conform.

If Hindu people come to believe that their faith in Jesus makes it impossible for them to participate in the dharmic culture of covenantal relationship within their extended family, and if they decide to align with the Christians on that basis, they have literally broken covenant with their family. They have not only spurned their privileges and responsibilities as a member of that family, but they have actually lost the right to live among their people. The family interprets their actions as a decision to keep covenant with other families and jatis—that is, Christians—and that throws them into turmoil, because now they do not know how to relate to their family member appropriately. The result is that the new believer is de facto out of the community. Any explicit breech of relationship with the believing family member is simply a formal recognition of what already exists—a broken covenant.

The "conversion" approach to discipleship may even rise to the level of betrayal, because the "converts" may have greatly damaged the ability of their family members who have not confessed Christ to keep covenant with the other families of their clan, jati, or caste. Everybody in the social world of the new believer's family will quickly come to know that the new believer is now in covenant with Christians, which damages the reputation of the entire family. This level of conflict and angry reaction doesn't always happen, but it happens often enough.

Furthermore, and tragically, the inability or unwillingness of the converts to live within this covenantal culture has made it impossible for them to have any influence for Christ among their own people. "We gain one and lose a hundred." One of the major reasons for this is that disciples of Jesus who bring the gospel to Hindus have failed to deal with the covenantal nature of these relationships. Foreign Christians have been largely unaware of these dynamics, because Hindu culture is so different from their culture, and Indian Christians have insisted that the converts live covenantally with *them*.

There must be a concerted, focused network of effort to try to understand how Hindus can continue to live covenantally with their families, not compromise the lordship of Christ, and even have influence for Christ within the family and jati. Obviously, Hindu believers themselves must develop this. That is what makes it a truly insider approach.

Although we long to see Hindu disciples of Jesus live covenantally with their extended Hindu family, there are heartbreaking situations in which it is virtually impossible for them to do so. This happens when their devotion to Jesus has so upset the elders or other power players in the family that they decide to break covenant with the disciple. The Hindu disciple of Christ wants to live covenantally with their people, but the family rejects them. Even at this point, however, some compromise and wise relational barriers may allow a long-term, if imperfect, relationship to be maintained.

If the wider family does not respond to this, insisting instead that the new believer recant faith in Christ, then the believer should be encouraged and supported by other people, who will help them adjust to this new reality of living apart from their family as a disciple of Jesus. Even so, great care must be taken to develop a lifestyle that will not make future reconciliation with the family impossible. The very best counselors in such situations are other Hindu disciples of Jesus and, if necessary, a few Christians who are sensitive and experienced.

If discipleship to Jesus means that the Hindu believer must break covenant with his or her family, Hindus will continue to view Christianity—and by extension, Christ himself—as a real threat to the Hindu community. Sadly, this reality is all too common, and it is the exact opposite of good news for the world.

THE VERSES

There has been significant misunderstanding and misapplication of the portions of Scripture that speak to devotion to Jesus and human relationships—family in particular. These verses are sometimes used irresponsibly to justify advising Hindu people to leave their family if the family is not open to their new relationship with Jesus. This is such a widespread problem that we must look carefully at how to use these scriptures correctly in discipling situations with Hindus.

Perhaps the one used the most is Matthew 10:37—"Anyone who loves his father or mother more than me is not worthy of me; anyone who loves his son or daughter more than me is not worthy of me." However, as the previous verse makes clear ("A man's enemies will be the people of his own household"), this passage is in fact an application of Micah 7:1–6.

The passage in Micah refers to a time of great apostasy and sin. The society was filled with violence and corruption. Bribery of and by leaders was rife. Sin was so pervasive that the faithful were oppressed because they did not act like everybody around them. Often a man's enemies were the very people he loved and who he thought loved him. A man's own family and friends were persecuting him because he did not rush into sin with everyone else. The first six verses of Micah 7 state these facts. Then verse 7 testifies to how the faithful respond to a society given over to sin, when they face persecution from friends and even family because they do not join in their sin. The faithful must wait on the Lord, trusting him for deliverance and revival.

Jesus uses this passage of Scripture in Matthew 10 to make a powerful point about faithfulness. He means to apply the situation described in Micah 7 to encourage his disciples to be faithful no matter what they encounter, even if the persecution comes from the family—which no doubt it will. The teaching is about faithfulness in and through situations that test our faith, especially when it happens within our family. This is possible if the disciples are living in union with Jesus Christ, trusting him for deliverance and spiritual revival of the people around them.

It is a bad interpretation, and a worse application, to use Matthew 10:37 to teach that walking away from your Hindu family is the price of devotion to Jesus. These scriptures are actually saying the exact opposite! The family may tempt, persecute, or even abandon the disciple of Jesus, but the disciple does not abandon the family. He or she is aware of the risks, accepts the hardship and persecution, is supported by others who believe in Christ, and faithfully waits on the Lord for deliverance and for the revival of the family, as Micah 7:7 says.

Luke 14:25–26 is another passage that is used by Christians to advise Hindus to walk away from their families: "Now large crowds were traveling with him; and he turned and said to them, 'Whoever comes to me and does not hate father and mother, wife and children, brothers and sisters, yes, and even life itself, cannot be my disciple. Whoever does not carry the cross and follow me cannot be my disciple.'" Hindu people will completely understand this scripture. In fact, Christians need *Hindus* to explain it to *them*, because it has been significantly reduced by global Christianity to mean that "converts" should attend church even if their parents or family disapprove.

These verses are an example of how Jesus taught people about bhakti, or devotion to him. He uses hyperbole to make a strong point. Obviously he is not telling us to literally hate our parents. That would be completely at odds with God's will. Rather, Jesus is saying that discipleship to him involves the entire person, everything one has. It is a significant reduction to teach that this verse is fulfilled by going to a church in spite of what one's Hindu family thinks, as if churches always live up to this teaching about devotion. Of course they don't.

When Hindu disciples encounter this passage from Luke, it should bring to mind echoes of Hindu myths and legends such as the stories of Radha and Krishna, and the teachings of their gurus and saints. Hindu lore and teaching is filled with stories about this level of bhakti and a similar type of hyperbole in communication. Hindus will be skilled in interpreting and applying this scripture to life.

There is clear risk of persecution, which Jesus underscores by mentioning the possibility of crucifixion, and persecution is exactly what Hindus would expect from devotion to Jesus. However, it is absolutely incorrect to use this to justify walking away from family to join the Christian community.

Another scripture that is used to pressure Hindus to walk away from their family is Mark 3:31–34: "Then his mother and his brothers came; and standing outside, they sent to him and called him. A crowd was sitting around him; and they said to him, 'Your mother and your brothers and sisters are outside, asking for you.' And he replied, 'Who are my mother and my brothers?' And looking at those who sat around him, he said, 'Here are my mother and my brothers!'"

In this scripture, Jesus uses a tense moment of conflicting expectations with his mother and siblings to explain the measure of his love. He is not saying that his disciples have replaced his family. Instead, he is saying that the best way to explain the depth and width of love that he has for his disciples is to compare it to the love he has for his family. The love and devotion that he has for the latter shows us how he feels about the former. Thus Jesus is actually exalting the family as the model of faith and love rather than saying that his disciples have superseded them. Again, using this scripture to justify a break with family to follow Jesus is inappropriate.

Another scripture that is used by Christians to extract Hindus from their community is 2 Corinthians 6:14—"Do not be unequally yoked with unbelievers. For what partnership has righteousness with lawlessness? Or what fellowship has light with darkness?"

Most Christians think this scripture is about marriage. Some even apply it to any sort of partnership, such as business. The interpretation is as follows: Since the clearest and most common example of being yoked, being in partnership, and having fellowship is marriage, it is therefore always wrong for a believer in Christ to marry an unbeliever. The believer lives in the righteous light of Jesus, the unbeliever in the lawless darkness of unbelief. Being "unequally yoked" must refer to a marriage between these two types of people.

Christians often use this scripture as the basis for counseling a Hindu person who is a disciple of Christ to decline a marriage proposal with a person who is not a disciple of Christ. Frequently, this will be an arranged marriage between families in the same birth community, or jati. This is still how the majority of Hindu people get married, and it will be this way for many years to come, even though secularization continues to grow in India and among the Hindu diaspora. In many cases, there is no real way to get married without an arrangement that includes one's family.

If the Hindu disciple of Christ accepts the proposal and marries the person whom their parents have picked, Christians believe them to be unequally yoked—in direct violation of 2 Corinthians 6:14—no matter the circumstances or issues surrounding the decision. While there is no need to explain here why a marriage is greatly enhanced and blessed when the partners both share devotion to Jesus as the basis for how they live, we must acknowledge that this scripture is not directly related to marriage. It need not be used to encourage a Hindu disciple of Christ to decline an arranged marriage proposal.

Paul could have easily written this verse to a Hindu audience. In fact, much of both epistles to the Corinthians reads like that. This particular scripture, in its context, addresses the need for disciples who come from a polytheistic, idolatrous religious and cultural background to grow in wholehearted and single-minded devotion to Christ. The new believers in the Greek city of Corinth lived in a polytheistic environment filled with pagan religious practices. Some of the practices in the local temples, which these new believers certainly must have visited, were clearly of darkness, including ritualized prostitution. As children of light, for disciples of Christ to continue to be involved in this type of dark worship was certainly lawless. It was being "unequally yoked" with people still in darkness. As the Corinthians responded to the gospel, there was a consistent need to encourage the new disciples to follow Christ exclusively. Therefore, this verse should not be applied to the normal situation of Indian cultural marriage in which Hindu disciples of Christ find themselves.

This interpretation becomes clear when we read 2 Corinthians 6:14 in its context, which includes verses 15–18, where Paul quotes from Isaiah 52:11,

> What accord has Christ with Belial, or what portion does a believer share with an unbeliever? What agreement has the temple of God with idols? For we are the temple of the living God; as God said, "I will make my dwelling among them and walk among them, and I will be their God, and they shall be my people. Therefore go out from their midst, and be separate from them, says the Lord, and touch no unclean thing; then I will welcome you, and I will be a father to you, and you shall be sons and daughters to me, says the Lord Almighty."

The entire context of these verses is very clear about the need for disciples of Christ to avoid the dark, idolatrous practices of the Greek temples in Corinth and focus exclusively on devotion to Christ. This passage deeply challenges Hindu people along the lines of an exclusive relationship with Jesus. There is no hint of applying this scripture to teach the "sin" of accepting a proposal of marriage that one's parents have arranged or approved on one's behalf. That is another manmade reduction of this very powerful and even confrontational verse.

If 2 Corinthians 6:14 does not refer to marriages of disciples from Hindu background with Hindus who are not disciples, then how do we approach the issue of these types of marriages? Is any marriage acceptable, regardless of faith in Christ? Certainly not! Marriage is the very first institution God gave humanity, and it is by far the most important factor in anyone's life. The decision to enter into marriage with someone should always be considered carefully, biblically, and even fearfully. A good marriage is wonderful. A bad marriage is a dreadful, soul-shattering experience.

Discipleship is never more collaborative than when we consider marriage and family. It is vital for us to help Hindus who are disciples of Christ know God's intentions, desires, and values concerning marriage. The Bible is filled with rich teachings about marriage. Hindu disciples of Christ should be encouraged and challenged by all of them, for these teachings now belong to them just as much as they do to Christians. The mentor helps the Hindu disciples interpret and apply these biblical teachings about marriage to their personal lives and cultural context rather than telling them what to do or not do and who to marry or not marry. Of course, a marriage that will make these values unsustainable is ill-advised and should be avoided if at all possible.

The ideal scenario is when the Hindu disciple's parents request help in understanding how Jesus views marriage from Scripture; then the mentor has a chance to respond. The family may do this because they want what's best for the individual family member, who is now a follower of Jesus, as well as for their entire family. However, they will only make such a request if an authentic, sustainable relationship has been the mentor's goal from the very beginning. And the mentor must be very sensitive when giving input on this issue, always bearing in mind that there are boundaries to the request. The relevant passage of Scripture must simply be pointed out to the family. The mentor should help them interpret it but never tell them how to apply it—unless explicitly asked. This is a Bible-based, Christ-centered approach to the frequently controversial area of marriage and faith in Christ.

If a Hindu disciple of Christ comes from a family that is secular and modern, then they may already have quite a bit of freedom to marry whoever they want. In this context, the example of the apostle Paul in 1 Corinthians 7 is very helpful. There were those in Corinth who had to resolve some complex issues concerning marriage, and it seems that they approached Paul for guidance. Paul replied, in essence, "This is how I see it: do the best you can to make Christ-centered decisions about the various marriage issues you are dealing with, always looking to please the Lord." In the spirit of that advice, it is best for people who have freedom from traditional cultural constraints to avoid marriage to someone who is not a disciple of Christ and to marry any disciple of Christ from any community they wish, including the Christian community. It's okay to have a "love marriage" with another disciple of Christ!

Again, in the spirit of 1 Corinthians 7, if circumstances are such that the disciples do not seem to have any marriage prospects, and if they know that their parents are grieving over this situation, they may decide that the Lord wants them to discuss with their parents the possibility of marriage to someone whom their parents find for them. The rationale for assuming that God wants them to do this is the very clear value that God places throughout Scripture on obeying one's parents. Their parents' instincts about the blessing of marriage will be pleasing to the Lord, and the parents probably already realize that their child, who is now a disciple of Christ, will only marry someone who allows and unambiguously supports their devotion to Christ.

It is also probably best for the believer to inform their parents that they intend to live separately with their spouse rather than within a practicing Hindu family, which would likely prove to be difficult in the long run and could eventually cause the marriage to break down. Living separately also allows the disciple of Christ the freedom to teach the gospel to their children. This approach to marriage is a 1 Corinthians 7 type of compromise, but it can be done in the right way. Beyond doubt, the very best option is always for believers in Christ to marry another believer.

The scriptures quoted above, and others like them, are often used to convince Hindu devotees of Jesus to ignore or even leave their families. This interpretation is completely wrong. The passages actually teach the opposite: Jesus wants Hindu people to remain in their family, even enduring persecution to do so! He is calling them to an extraordinary level of faithful seva and bhakti rather than fleeing into an extracted Christian environment.

Living as a disciple of Jesus within a Hindu family is not always easy to understand. There are no easy answers, nor is there a manageable list of do's and don'ts. It is the heart attitude of bhakti and seva that means everything. Jesus said that dharma is captured by loving God with one's whole being and then loving everybody else with the same love that the disciple needs. This foundational value informs everything.

DISCIPLESHIP PATTERNS

In popular culture, the word "disciple" usually implies some sort of "religious follower." It is also connected to the word "discipline" when the latter is used to mean a subject of study or a way of life that is focused on a goal. In the Bible, the concept of discipleship, becoming a disciple, is derived from the Greek word *mathetes*, which means "learner" or "student." A disciple is simply a student of Jesus, someone who learns from Jesus.

What exactly do we learn from Jesus? We learn how to do everything he teaches us, as he has commanded in Matthew 28:18–20, translating his teachings into our present time. In other words, we come to understand what Jesus taught his disciples, and we develop the skills to put that same teaching into practice in our life. That is the essence of discipleship.

Discipleship is used in church life to mean growth in some manner as a Christian. Just about every Christian denomination uses it, but the practice of discipleship varies greatly based on the distinctive doctrine and practice of the denomination or local church. Ironically, there is no real consensus about what a Christian disciple looks like, and even less consensus about how to actually implement discipleship. The last two thousand years of church history have made Christian consensus about most things virtually impossible.

This uncertainty about discipleship is rather disturbing, because we discover in the New Testament narratives that Jesus made disciples a lot. He had many disciples. He started with five men, and then he added to this number until twelve men and a group of influential women became his disciples. Then, he added seventy more until there were 120 people who were his disciples, including his family members, by the time he ascended into heaven. Discipleship was what Jesus did, so we must be and make disciples too.

The typical assumptions about making disciples who are Protestant, Catholic, Orthodox, or Anglican can introduce significant problems when we begin to think about discipleship in a Hindu context. If discipleship is intertwined with being a good Christian of a certain variety, then how do we make disciples of Hindus? Is discipleship only for people who have Christian identity? This bring us back to the very real dilemma of whether Hindu people may follow Jesus as Hindus or whether they must leave their birth community and become Christians in order to become disciples. There is a great deal of confusion about this issue, and it's undoubtedly a difficult one. Having wrestled with this question myself, and having worked among Hindu people over a number of years, I believe that Hindus can be disciples of Jesus. In fact, they *must* become disciples of Jesus.

How does the obvious complexity of being a Hindu person who is surrendering to Jesus Christ as Savior and Lord impact discipleship? Perhaps I can answer that with an illustration.

One day I was sitting in my office, preparing to lead a Bible study with a group of Hindu people. Some were already believers in Jesus, others were just exploring what that meant, but all of them were very open to the Lord Jesus. As I prayed about the study, asking God to help me understand what approach to take, the Holy Spirit spoke to me plainly: "Teach this as if the last two thousand years of church history never happened. It never happened for them."

That was a seminal moment for me. As I meditated on this "word of wisdom" from God over the following days and weeks, I realized that I needed to start over. I needed to discover how to make disciples in direct connection to Jesus, apart from all of the Christian clutter. The inherent danger in this approach was that I would make a lot of mistakes at the expense of the Hindu people even as I learned about discipleship apart from church history. Worse, it could mean that I would begin making disciples of *myself*! But because God's word was so clear, I adopted a collaborative approach.

I decided to work together with the people I was discipling so that all of us could experience discipleship together. This meant that I pointed them to Jesus, mostly in the context of the Bible, and as a group we tried to understand what we were discovering as we interacted with our Lord about how to become his disciples. Over time, a philosophy of discipleship emerged that changed not only the lives of some Hindu people but my own life as well.

DISCIPLESHIP IN A HINDU CONTEXT

I have learned several lessons through the collaborative approach to ministry in the Hindu context. I hope you will find them helpful.

1. Discipling as Coaches. We must disciple Hindu people as coaches rather than as teachers. It is very important to make sure they believe that they can learn directly from Jesus. The people with whom the Hindus have been experiencing Jesus must simply come alongside and help them continue to learn from Jesus. We found that coaching in this way needs to be done within a group of people who all want to follow Christ, or who are at least very seriously and humbly looking into that. A mixed group of bhaktas and onlookers leads to endless rabbit trails and arguments that are not helpful.

This coaching method takes multiple forms. Growing disciples need several vital ingredients: the motivation to prayerfully and carefully read the Gospel narratives; inspiration to trust the working of the Holy Spirit, who will teach them how to apply what they learn in their daily lives; and encouragement to try to articulate what they are learning. We must also suggest how the Gospels were a fulfillment of the Old Testament, and how these great sections of Scripture were contextualized in the book of Acts. This will lead growing Hindu disciples of Jesus to explore the Bible further, for obviously the events in the book of Acts are the context for the New Testament epistles. Open discussion of what all of this may look like in their own world is extremely important.

The ability to work together with Hindu disciples to solve problems and deal with issues, while resisting the temptation to be the "Bible answer man or woman," is essential. Hindus must know that we trust them, that we believe in them, and they must develop confidence to follow Jesus according to the example they have learned from those with whom they have been experiencing Jesus. This is how the process is more like coaching than teaching.

2. Bhakti and Seva. We must also emphasize the complementary focus of being and doing—becoming like Christ and doing what he did. This incorporates both bhakti and seva. The first apprentices of Jesus did these two things simultaneously. They learned the gospel very deeply so they could be faithful, and they learned how to do the ministry of the gospel like Jesus did so they would be fruitful. They would listen to Jesus teach the gospel to one person or to large crowds, and on the same day they would accompany him as he healed people, drove out evil spirits, encouraged families, or prayed to God for miracles. They learned the vital truth that enabled them to stay faithful in the gospel, and at the same time they learned kingdom ministry skills in order to be fruitful in their ministry. This is the genius of Jesus, and it is our model for making disciples in the Hindu context. So what does this philosophy of bhakti and seva look like in Hindu disciples' lives?

The authentic relationship between the Hindu and non-Hindu disciples of Jesus continues and deepens. Everyone is given room to breathe, to live, so these unique relationships never usurp the place of the family. This enables Hindus to keep covenant relationship with their family according to how they interpret and live out the dharmic Hindu calendar. In this respect, every family is a little different, so one can expect variations.

The believers in Christ, both Hindu and non-Hindu, support each other, care about each other, and are growing to understand each other. Each helps the other to understand how a disciple lives faithfully and fruitfully within their culture, or the fusion of culture in which they live. There is a value of slowly and surely introducing one another to the important people in our lives so that devotion to Jesus can be integrated into the real world.

At this point a way to gather together for bhakti and seva, worship and service, has been devised. It is led by the Hindu people. The non-Hindu believers have gently refused to take over, but have helped the Hindu people develop the skills they need to lead the gathering. This may be referred to as a satsang. It may be an organized gathering that happens regularly or an organic event that happens from time to time. The goal of the gathering is to continue to come to clarity and depth of relationship with God by experiencing the benevolent power of Jesus through prayer and worship. In addition to satsang, the disciples look for ways to serve people outside of the satsang gathering. Needs will be readily apparent, for there are always needs within and among people everywhere. Learning how to bless people in need will gradually become clear.

The gospel continues to be uncovered and processed in Bible study. People read the Bible on their own or gather together in some way, either in a satsang or informally, to discuss what they learn. The Gospel narratives are the core of the study. The Hindus are constantly exploring how Jesus fulfilled the Old Testament and how the rest of the New Testament describes the incarnated kingdom of God, and applying these insights to their lives.

3. Translation of Scripture. Translating the Scripture into the life of Hindu people will be a significant part of discipleship within a

Hindu context. Translation is a basic function of the gospel ministry and one of the unique characteristics of the Christian faith. The reason we translate rather than exporting one transcultural church that looks exactly the same everywhere is that, at its core, Christianity is not a set of doctrines and practices. It is the company of people who believe in the Lord Jesus Christ, and who are joined to him by the Holy Spirit. At the center of the gospel is Jesus. This is crucial, because without a Christ-centered discipleship, the dangers of syncretism will constantly plague any attempt to translate the gospel into the life of a Hindu disciple of Christ.

Many people who love the Lord and love Hindu people have been unwilling to translate the gospel into Hindu forms because they fear syncretism. I can understand that—but syncretism and translation are not the same thing. Syncretism is a third thing, a new entity that people create when they try to combine incompatible things. For example, saying that Christ and Krishna are the same, each one the true incarnation of God for different cultures, is syncretism. Jesus and Krishna are not the same. Following one is not the functional equivalent of following the other, because Jesus Christ is the center of the gospel. One cannot translate Jesus into Krishna. When we lose Jesus, we lose everything.

The gospel in all of its fullness has been translated into cultures and languages all over the world. The New Testament and church history teach us that the Spirit has always worked without reference to any dominant tradition, but he joins people with Christ from every culture in the world. This is why translation of the gospel glorifies God.

There is ongoing research and dialogue about how to translate the life of the kingdom of God into Hindu culture. Syncretism is not viewed as an either-or mistake indicating an ultimate lack of faith in Christ, but rather as *a point along a line*. In other words, we expect growing quality and accuracy in the application of the gospel in the Hindu world; there will be progress and movement toward a truer expression. Therefore we need not panic when we encounter syncretism.

For example, suppose the new disciples try hard to translate the powerful scriptures about costly discipleship (explained above) into their Hindu family. They take initiative to love and serve their parents and grandparents, listening to their advice about life. They understand the financial expectations that the family has for individual members, and they do not abandon those commitments, especially if everybody else is keeping them. The disciples listen to their family's point of view—which might include grievances—about this new lifestyle of bhakti and seva to Jesus. The disciples pray about all of these things, asking God in Jesus' name for wisdom to see the clear path of bhakti before them. It is important in this process that foreigners, and even Indian Christians, do not apply pressure when decisions have to be made; all they can do is provide information from Scripture and coach the disciple to make good decisions.

Even though it might feel strange initially, it is possible to live this way. But know this: discipling Hindu people who choose a lifestyle of bhakti and seva among their family will change *your* life. In fact, it may even turn your world upside down!

An example of translation from the Gospels is the discipleship pattern that Jesus followed. The way that he taught his disciples was an apprenticeship model. He was the master, and his disciples were apprentices who would learn how to be like him and do what he was able to do because they lived with him. In the Jewish context, this apprenticeship culture of learning was part of the rabbinical system. A rabbi, or teacher, had students who stayed near him, and he taught them to imitate his lifestyle and ministry. The disciples learned from Rabbi Jesus by being with him.

The word for rabbi in Indian languages and Hindu culture is *guru*. The disciples or learners are his *shishya*. The model for learning from a guru is similar to the apprenticeship model in the Jewish rabbinical system. The guru chooses his apprentice followers, who develop his character and skill. Thus, it is perfectly correct to say that Jesus is our guru and we are learning from him. *Guru* is a sound translation of "rabbi" into Hindu culture. In fact, Bible translations in Indian languages such as Gujarati use the word *guru* for teacher or rabbi when referring to Jesus.

We have suggested that Jesus translated the rabbinical system of apprenticeship into his kingdom ministry of discipleship. Now we will go a step further and suggest that it is appropriate to translate the name and title "Lord Jesus Christ" into words from the Hindu world that mean the same thing and that accurately represent him according to Scripture and history.

We must remember that "Lord Jesus Christ" is itself a Hellenized translation of Jesus' Hebrew name and title, *Yeshua Ha Mashiach*. Both the Greek and the original Hebrew mean "The Anointed Lord of Salvation." Our suggested translation in the Hindu context is *Muktidatta Abhishikta*. *Muktidatta* means "Lord of Salvation" and *Abhishikta* means "Anointed as King." Thus, *Muktidatta Abhishikta* means "the Anointed King who is the Lord of Salvation." Yeshua Ha Mashiach, Lord Jesus Christ, and Muktidatta Abhishikta all mean the same thing. Therefore, it is fully appropriate for Hindu people who are learning to be faithful in the gospel and fruitful in the ministry of the gospel to tell people that they are "bhaktas of Guruji Muktidatta Abhishikta," which is a translation of the term "Christian."

Finally, another major issue of translation is how to practice *sadhana*, or the spiritual disciplines. Things like fasting, meditation, focused worship, and solitude are invaluable for healing our battered and wounded souls and growing to become like Jesus. Many Hindus have extensive knowledge or experience around spiritual disciplines that should be redeemed by the gospel and applied to their lives. Thus it becomes imperative to study how Jesus did sadhana and then translate that into Hindu culture.

CHURCH, BAPTISM, AND THE LORD'S SUPPER

Hindus struggle in their relationship to the church, and vice versa. The global church, including conversion-oriented evangelicals and traditional denominations, is obviously focused on Christians and the practice of Christianity. Since Hindus are not Christians, relationship between Hindus and these types of churches fluctuates between polite indifference and open conflict. However, the reign of God in Jesus Christ extends to both groups. This reality of God's reign, or his kingdom, is the foundation upon which any attempt at relationship between Hindus and the global church must be built. A church should be understood in light of the kingdom rather than the kingdom being understood in light of a church.

As we have said before, the kingdom of God is the *rule* or *reign* of God. It is his king*ship*, his activity as king. The kingdom of God includes all of God's activity from the beginning of time—including creation, the flow and purpose of history, the rise and fall of human government and power, and the birth, life, and death of every individual who has ever lived. The rule and reign of God is fully comprehensive, and because God is good, his reign as king is benevolent and just. The church—local congregations as well as the various translocal or even global denominations—is a part of the kingdom, but the kingdom is not limited to the church. God ruled before the church came into existence, and he continues to rule over everyone and everything, both within the church and outside its sphere of influence. His reign goes beyond the church and includes Hindu civilization.

God has ordained that millions of people would be born into Hindu families and live as Hindus. This means that he has no more of an issue with Hindus than he does with any other people who are diminished because of their experience of personal and societal sin. He loves Hindus and accepts them without requiring them to participate in the culture of the global church.

This also means that believers can enter Hindu communities anywhere on earth and help them experience Jesus in a Hindu-friendly way. Hindu disciples of Jesus can be as confident of God's favor as other believers would be in their own cultural communities. Furthermore, Hindus may live as fully devoted disciples of Jesus without worrying that their birth and lifestyle as Hindus prevent them from experiencing life as learners from Jesus, the essence of what it means to be a disciple. Finally, the fact that God loves and accepts Hindus means that churches which emerge from inside Hindu culture are not only acceptable but actually preferable.

Churches do not have the right or authority to impose their traditions on Hindus who are surrendering to the reign of God through faith in Jesus Christ, because the kingdom of God supersedes the discipline of churches. This means that no one has to defer to churches that hinder the spread of the gospel, and certainly no one must persecute Hindus who are coming to Jesus by callously trying to extract them from their family into a church. Church membership is not the point. Discipleship to Jesus is the point.

Since established churches are much further down the discipleship road than groups of new believers, they are called by God to support Hindus so they may grow as disciples of Jesus. Paul's letter to the Galatians teaches that churches have freedom to innovate how they function: "You, my brothers, were called to be free. But do not use your freedom to indulge the sinful nature; rather, serve one another in love. The entire law is summed up in a single command: 'Love your neighbor as yourself'" (Galatians 5:14–15). Following this teaching will allow the gospel of grace to spread widely and deeply among Hindus. The sacraments of baptism and the Lord's Supper don't have to be stumbling blocks for Hindu people, but that is often exactly what happens. It is important to implement them well, weaving together biblical integrity and local culture. If the Hindu disciples decide to enter into Christ-centered covenant relationship with a local Christian community, there may eventually be value in observing the sacraments in a way that conforms to traditional Christian practice—but that is not the goal.

Baptism can be a huge problem for Hindu people because of how it has been implemented by churches in India and around the world throughout history. Biblical examples of baptism have usually been interpreted and applied by many in Christendom, or Christendom-model churches in India, to mean identification with the church. Some groups of Christians believe baptism is essentially becoming a Christian. It is also very common for Christians to insist that only ordained ministers—who are therefore authorized agents of the church—be allowed to baptize people.

Typical church-centered baptism has always meant changing one's religion to Christianity and keeping covenantal relationship with other Christians. This approach to baptism works well for local church-based ministry among Christians. It is also easy to implement with new believers in Christ who are free to associate with people as they wish. But assuming that baptism can and should be practiced in this manner among Hindus is a mistake. It is an example of seeing the kingdom through a church lens rather than seeing the church through a kingdom lens.

The rite of baptism can be translated into Hindu culture as a *sanskaar*, which means purification. It is therefore a sacred or dharmic ceremony. Disciples of Jesus observe this sanskaar of water baptism as a symbol of our union with Christ in his death and resurrection. Since his death and resurrection have purified and washed us from sin, baptism fits perfectly into the idea of a sanskaar. We may refer to baptism as *jal sanskaar* (water rite) or *guru diksha* (initiation of the guru). Using these Hindu terms helps to reduce the tremendous baggage that the English word carries.

Translating baptism as a sanskaar for the Hindu world requires that we disconnect it from the church and Christian culture and instead connect it to salvation through Jesus Christ. It is imperative for Hindus to be baptized in ways that help their families and friends believe that they have become disciples of Jesus Christ and now wish to observe the sanskaar of water baptism as a testimony to their salvation from sin. This sanskaar also indicates their desire to be a bhakta of Jesus. In this spirit, it is best for Hindus to baptize one another. Of course, the Hindus who lead the sanskaar are bhaktas of Jesus.

We must take the same approach with the Lord's Supper, disconnecting it from the institutional church and connecting it to

Jesus. To do this we must study Scripture together with the new disciples thoroughly. They will have questions about this sanskaar, which we must discuss clearly, freely, and graciously. The point is to help the new disciples create a way to observe the Lord's Supper for themselves, so that they will be inspired to contextualize it in a way that clarifies the lordship of Christ, who died, was raised, and will return to earth. Once they understand this, we must encourage them to lead the group of disciples who are worshipping in celebrating this sanskaar.

The sanskaar of the Lord's Supper can be observed with any adult Hindus who say they understand the meaning of it, whether they are baptized or not. Their frame of reference will be that this is a *prasad*, or food offered to God, blessed by God, and then redistributed to people. In this way, many Hindus feel they are touched by God's grace. They will want to develop their own manner of doing it, and then do it that way each time. This will speak to them very deeply and draw them even closer to Jesus.

CONCLUSION

Discipleship is what Jesus did. We are never more like him than when we are growing as disciples and making disciples. Hindus can be fully devoted disciples of Jesus. In fact, the quality and intensity of their bhakti and seva may surprise you!

Often Christians assume that Hindus who are fully devoted disciples of Christ will be more like them and less like typical Hindu people—for example, that they will know how to participate in a local church small group or a Bible study; that they will be comfortable in a worship service on Sunday; that they will feel aligned or connected to the local Christian community; or that their children will marry Christians. It is wonderful if all of that happens, especially if it is freely chosen by the Hindu people. However, that way of life is not the best choice if the Hindus are extracted out of their Hindu community and have little or no positive influence for Christ among other Hindus. What needs to be seen is that Hindus may be fully devoted disciples without necessarily feeling comfortable or participating in the Christian culture.

Making disciples in a Hindu context will change your life for the better, but it will also make it more difficult. If you are privileged to go through this with Hindu people, you may find that your experience of church-based Christianity, in which structured discipleship is an option, leaves you feeling unsatisfied and even unsettled. You may be shocked by the misinformation that circulates about Hindu people, and negative perception people have of following Jesus within a non-Christian environment or discipleship within a family.

I have found that it is best to ask God for some meaningful relationships with disciples from one's own culture, those who subscribe to a life of discipleship rather than focusing on significant church involvement. Staying connected to a church can be a good thing. Resolve to be a source of joy to other people, without getting involved in the conflicts and controversy that tend to beset the local church. It is also good to contribute to the church's program in at least one significant way. Such a connection will provide stability for yourself and your family while at the same time allowing you to witness the miracle of seeing Hindus come to Christ.

CHAPTER 7

THE DISCIPLE MAKER

MAKING DISCIPLES within Hindu families will change us, but not in the ways we may assume. We will not have to become masterful apologists who have every answer to every question the Hindu mind has ever conceived. We will not have to become vegetarians or learn how to drape a sari. We will not have to meditate for hours or develop a penchant for incense. You may do all of these and more if you like, but none of them will determine if you can make disciples within Hindu families and communities. Don't worry. You can stay pretty much as you are, with one exception: you will need to focus your life on a deep and wide relationship with Christ. In other words, you will need to become a disciple of Christ yourself.

Disciples are faithful and fruitful. They are faithful to the gospel, understanding the good news deeply, experientially, and opening up their life completely to the lordship of Christ. They are fruitful in that they do the same things Jesus did, which naturally involves developing the skills necessary to do everything he demonstrated and taught. Fruitfulness is simply what Jesus does within you and through you, the theme of his great sermon in John 15.

This faithfulness and fruitfulness will need to characterize the life of someone who makes disciples within Hindu families.

We must always remember that disciples of Christ will face opposition and discouragement in a ministry of this kind, but our adversary is Satan, not the people themselves. It is easy to think that Hindus are the problem, or that the problem is with us or with the Christian community. This is also the blinding, stifling work of Satan. We must never forget that he is at the bottom of it all. At the end of the day, *he* is the problem.

Satan blinds Hindus to the true identity of Jesus and keeps disciple-making believers from recognizing the freedom they must embrace to bring a Christ-centered gospel to their Hindu friends, a gospel that is unadulterated with tradition. He blinds local Christians to the centrality of Christ so that they will stay preoccupied with the traditions, institutions, and boundaries of Christianity. Satan also brings heavy, smothering layers of confusion and condemnation to disciple makers and Hindus who are trying to experience Jesus together. This is why Satan is the one we have to fight, and we do that in prayer. We must ask Jesus to lift the black fog of doubt and confusion in our mind and to break the deception that Satan is wielding, through which both Hindus and Christians are blinded to the person of Christ.

You will have to assess the risk of moving this life of discipleship away from your particular Christian center and directing it toward Hindu people. It is indeed risky. Your Christian friends may wonder why you miss so many small group gatherings or ask why you are eating dinner with your new Indian friends. Since Sunday is the best day to spend time with Hindu families, you may miss church from time to time. People may begin to pray for you because they are afraid you are abandoning the gathering together of the saints. After all, you are supposed to do that *more* as a disciple, not less.

As for Indian Christians—assuming you know any—you may come to the jarringly counterintuitive conclusion that in general you cannot rely on their perspective to help you understand a good way to interact with Hindu people. Although some individual Indian Christians will be like gold in this regard, others will truly shock you with their advice. Thus, there is a risk that your faithful and fruitful life of discipleship among Hindus may put you at odds with other Christians. This is almost always an unexpected difficulty.

Over time, you may discover that you need to do something else that doesn't quite feel right: You may need to compartmentalize your life as a Christian from your life as a person making disciples within a Hindu family or community. You may need to live two separate lives in two completely different worlds. The reason why this may help you is that Hindu culture and the culture of the average Christian church are both closed communities, and neither will change to accommodate the other. They are mutually exclusive worlds, and a Christian who wants to be a part of both communities will need to separate their involvement and participation in each from the other. Of course, while such compartmentalization will help you stay in both communities, it will not be easy. It will introduce levels of stress and conflict that would not exist if you were not responding to God's leading to disciple Hindu people.

There may come a time when you believe that God wants you to transition away from one of these two closed communities in order to focus on a more integrated life within one of them. In fact, it will definitely happen at some point, and it is nothing to be alarmed at. However, breaking relationship with either community must be done only in the most extreme circumstances.

If you believe God wants you to discontinue the Hindu ministry and integrate more fully back into your Christian center, allow yourself some time to process what you have experienced while making disciples within a Hindu community. You may feel deep and unexpected emotion at what seems to be concluded, finished, or lost. You have traveled with God to his kingdom frontier—even if it was only across the street or down the hall—and you will never be the same for it. Cherish the privileges you have enjoyed, grieve the losses, forgive the offenses. You have been blessed to have had this experience.

On the other hand, if you believe God wants you to further disconnect from your Christian center and integrate more deeply with a growing group of Hindu disciples, schedule some phone calls or coffee shop chats to let your Christian friends know of your decision. Consider talking to the elders or pastor in your Christian community. You do not need their permission to serve God, but it is important to communicate with them so they are aware of what God is doing in your life. They deserve that from you, especially if they have blessed and supported you thus far. Many of them will continue to stand behind you in prayer and committed fellowship. Make sure to reflect on everything you have been given by this particular Christian community, thanking certain people for how they have contributed to your life, assuring them of your friendship and affection. You have been privileged to share in their lives, and they should be told so.

It is tempting to conclude this book by saying how wonderful it is to serve the Lord in the Hindu community, how you can be certain that everything will turn out all right. You may want to hear that Christians and Hindus will eventually love you, understand who you are, and appreciate what you do. You may want to be reassured that you will be at perfect peace, knowing that you have been entirely faithful and fruitful. You may even want to know that you will not feel regret about what you have done or shame about what you have left undone.

Sorry, dear friends—that is a fantasy. While this ministry will bring you much joy, and while you will experience the working of God in unique and wonderful ways, everything will *not* be perfect. You will have moments—or extended periods—in your life when you are certain that *nothing* is right. You will say or do exactly the wrong thing at exactly the wrong time. You will look a God-given opportunity in the eye and walk away in anxiety or confusion. You will try to be faithful and fruitful, and fail.

Now what?

I think the most important passage of Scripture about imperfect people like us—all of us making disciples within Hindu communities—is 1 Corinthians 13. The Bible's chapter on love makes a paradigm-shattering claim about making disciples. What Paul basically says in this passage is that our finely honed spiritual gifts, our knowledge of Hindu culture, and our disciple-making skills are not enough. We will fail, but we can overcome that inevitable failure by opening the deepest vaults of our soul to the love of God in Christ.

As we stay faithful to the gospel, even when it entails disappointment, heartache, or confusion, we learn how to love God and people with that same love. *That* is being fruitful. That love never fails. This is where hope and resilience come from, and it is the most important thing to remember. God bless you on your journey with Hindus.

मार्ग

APPENDIX

RHYTHMS

CONTACT DEVELOPMENT (CD) is a way for workers to conceive of and implement gospel-centered discipleship ministry within upper-caste Hindu communities anywhere in the world. Its purpose is to enable a group of Jesus followers to find the individuals—and hopefully the families—in whom God is already working, preparing them to receive the gospel.

When followers of Jesus live missionally among Hindus, they may eventually need to develop rhythms of lifestyle and ministry that position them to discover the patterns of how God is working among Hindu people. CD helps disciples build these rhythms into their life for that purpose.

The rhythms of CD help the disciples evaluate the level of risk and reward in ministry so that we can see areas of kingdom breakthrough in people's lives and take the risks that accompany that breakthrough. This will also help us avoid taking risks in ministry if we do not see potential that justifies the risk. When the reward is worth the risk, these rhythms help us discern the "space" that God is opening for the gospel to work within people's lives. We plant the seed of the gospel in that space, working in concert with God as he increases the room for the gospel to take root.

CD also helps us create assessment instruments that reveal fruitful approaches, natural relationships, and levels of receptivity. These instruments allow us to evaluate how well the workers are functioning, individually and as a team, in what can be a very subjective and relational ministry—one in which it is rather easy to get lost. Having metrics helps the community of Jesus followers avoid mediocrity on the one hand and discouragement on the other.

The rhythms of CD help the workers discover their individual strengths and weaknesses in this type of ministry. For example, a person who is gifted as a pastor may have a hard time making initial contacts but find it easier to teach and build up people later. Likewise, an evangelist may thrive at the beginning of an outreach-focused ministry but struggle with the pastoral care that new disciples need. The rhythms that CD provides are meant to guide people through such dilemmas.

There are five goals that build on one another. These goals are not achieved one by one and then set aside. They build upon one another as bricks are laid by a mason, forming a foundation of familiarity, trust, and influence that grows stronger over time. Each step of the process is designed to do one of two things. It either draws the Hindu family and the disciples of Christ closer together in authentic relationship so that they are experiencing Jesus together, or it allows the Hindu family to end the process in a way that enables a cordial relationship to continue. Both results are guaranteed in the course of ministry, and both should be considered successful outcomes, because in either case the worker has been faithful.

GETTING STARTED

Initiating ministry is often confusing and intimidating. It can be difficult, but it is not impossible. The chart below shows a step-by-step way to enter a Hindu community. Details will change according to the context, but the basic strategy is to find a public place where information about the activities of the local Hindu community is accessible; to discover points of common ground between the workers and the people; and to locate key people, known as *people of peace*, who can bring the workers into the Hindu world. The example given here is that of an Indian grocery store within a Hindu diaspora community. Once something like the four points below is completed, CD begins.

| 1. Explore the local area and find an Indian grocery store. All of the news about the Hindu community will be available there. | 2. Find out what local Hindus do that you enjoy. Then find a way to observe and eventually participate with them in that particular activity. | 3. You will be meeting people who do what you do and enjoy what you enjoy. Thus, you will be able to relate with them and they with you. | 4. Ask God to bring you a person of peace among these relationships. A person of peace accepts your identity as a disciple, introduces you to people, and invites you places. This will bring you further into the community. CD now begins. |

CONTACT DEVELOPMENT RHYTHMS

The five steps in CD are simply called CD1–5. The desired outcome of this process is to find Hindu people who are ready to listen to the gospel.

CD1. At this stage, Hindus invite the disciples into their lives. *They* pursue *you*. What does this look like? An invitation to their home or to a special event, eating lunch together at work, introducing you to friends—any of these would indicate acceptance. It's natural and authentic because it is a real relationship.

Even though CD1 is the first stage of CD, it is not the initial contact between a Hindu and a disciple. It is assumed that the disciples have already met Hindus and that some sort of relationship exists, as the chart above shows. Relationship does not always have to equate to genuine friendship. The rhythm of CD1 is that the Hindus understand and accept the identity that the disciples have in relation to them, and an authentic, honest, sustainable relationship is beginning. This is the initial stage of dealing with a person of peace.

Evaluation at this stage means asking the Lord to show you when and how this is happening. It may not take place as quickly as you expect, or it may be a more subtle kind of acceptance than you recognize. You must be prayerful. If after a period of time you sense that the Hindus are not responding with further openness, it is better to stay cordial and give priority to others who are more responsive. Allow people to move away from you, but pray for them privately, and always be friendly. These same people may have an individual, a family, or a community that they are preparing to receive you, while shaping you to receive them. Disciples must believe this. It is a matter of faith.

CD2. In this rhythm, the Hindus are accepting the disciples and opening their life up to them. By now the identity that the disciples want to have within the community—an identity that is socially and spiritually authentic and also makes sense to the Hindus—is understood. The disciples now want to move toward deeper levels of acceptance, so they invite the Hindus into *their* world. Disciples now do the pursuing. This back and forth makes sense to Hindus, who live within webs of covenant relationships in which they give and receive acceptance. At this stage disciples must invite them over and do something together—preferably something social.

The issue of food is a scary one for many vegetarians. Some Hindus do not eat or drink in any environment that is beyond their control, such as a restaurant or someone else's house. These are often higher caste people who are vegetarian as a matter of culture. If that is true, accept it and plan to spend much more time with them on their own turf, especially if they seem receptive to that and if they accept you more deeply over time.

Evaluation at this stage means that if after a period of time you sense that the Hindus have no interest in entering your life, you must ask God to reveal why this is so. The Hindus may simply be afraid to come into your world, or they may not want to risk any sort of misunderstanding or conflict if you do something they wouldn't do. Those of us who venture out of our cultural cocoon to incarnate our lives among Hindus tend to be far more culturally open than most people, including most Hindus, so we must not evaluate their actions based on our culture or level of comfort. As disciples of Christ we must not create impossible standards for others.

At the same time, we must not be unwilling to see things as they are. If your Hindu acquaintance will not enter your world at all, or if you realize that they are beginning to distance themselves, then you should consider whether they are trying to let you know that they are not interested in an authentic, sustainable relationship with a disciple of Christ. If that is what seems to be happening, don't try to force something that doesn't exist. Take the subtle hints and step away, maintaining a cordial public relationship.

CD3. This is the critical stage of experiencing Jesus. What does it look like? At this early stage, Jesus is experienced through answered prayer. As CD1 and CD2 happen, the disciples build trust. The Hindus may share a need or desire, which is an opportunity to pray. You can also ask them if you may pray for that need in Jesus' name—not privately, but with them. If they say yes, pray in Jesus' name in their presence. And of course do it on your own as well, when you can pray more freely and for a more extended period.

If the Lord so leads, and if there is openness, ask the Hindus to invite people over for the prayer. Arrange it with them, and make it a little ceremony. This happens if you believe that others will be open. When Hindus experience Jesus through an answered prayer, they become much more open to the gospel.

Evaluation at this stage means that if they decline your offer to pray, ask God to show you why. You may need to take it as a hint to keep things friendly and lengthen the relationship, or that you are rushing it, or that the Hindus are uncertain about the whole thing. The Spirit must show you what is going on. When the Hindus let you know something good happened because you prayed in Jesus' name, it may be time to explain why Jesus answered that prayer.

CD4. This is the stage to invite your Hindu friend to a worship time. There are some options on how to go about this. For instance, you can have a time of worship in the home to thank God for answering prayer, or you can invite them to a Bible study for Hindus or to a church service. You can also invite them to a small group meeting, a church plant, or a Christian holiday celebration like Easter or Christmas. If they come and enjoy it, great!

Evaluation at this stage means that if they do not come, you must seek to understand why. The venue may have been completely wrong, and greater thought should be given to creating worship events that appeal to Hindus. Things could stall even at this advanced point. God must show you, because at this level the stakes are obviously much higher than at CD1 or CD2. If everything went well, ask God to show you when and how to begin an evangelistic Bible study with them.

CD5. This is the stage when you all consider looking into the word of God about Jesus. If the Hindus agree, you move out of CD altogether into the Formal Evangelism stage. If they refuse, don't worry and don't rush. Don't force the issue. The stakes at CD5 are very high. Since you have already come so far, it is worth taking more time. Be willing to wait or walk, so to speak. Let them indicate the next step. Meanwhile keep praying for them.

If CD1 through CD4 is established in the relationship but your Hindu friends hesitate at CD5, be patient. However, if CD5 never happens and you start to realize that CD1 to CD4 is waning too, it may be time to let them move on. Whatever happens, do not break the relationship. Let them break it if they choose to do so, and always be cordial when you see them. Sometimes it seems you have come this far only to watch everything stall out. Do not be discouraged. You have planted good seed that may bear fruit down the road—you never know what might happen.

TRACKING MOVEMENT

Contact Development helps us keep track of ministry with individuals and families. We also use the chart on the next page to assess our total outreach. The idea is to track how Hindu people move forward from an initial contact to becoming a disciple of Christ. This helps solve many of the major problems that disciple makers face—problems such as whom to invest our time in; how to evaluate the effectiveness of our outreach; how to reach out to entire families; and how to end fruitless ministry. The chart is contextualized to Hindus and is based on how we have seen Hindus respond to the Holy Spirit.

As is evident from this chart, each category builds on the previous one and sets the stage for the next one. Begin by listing the names of people who fit each category, taking special note of relationships between people in different stages, especially within families. The first category will become very large as you continue to make contacts.

It is important to keep the list current. Thought must be given to how to move unresponsive people off of the chart in a way that is righteous and sensitive. We never want to become coldhearted about this.

Generally speaking, there will be a significant drop-off between CD1 and CD2. Several people will stop moving at CD3 as well. Don't worry. Just remain faithful and leave the rest to God.

BELIEVER: The Hindus who are embracing the lordship **6** of Jesus Christ over their present earthly lives and also over their lives after death. *CD4 to CD5*

BELIEVING: The Hindus who are **5** participating in ongoing worship and Bible study on the death and resurrection of Jesus Christ. *CD1 to CD5*

4 WORSHIP: The Hindus who are willing to worship Jesus. This is ongoing. *CD1 to CD4*

3 EXPERIENCE: The Hindus who positively accept an experience they have had with Jesus. *CD1 to CD3*

2 RELATIONSHIP: The Hindus with whom we have an authentic and sustainable relationship. *CD1 to CD2*

1 CONTACTS: A list of the Hindu people we have met and with whom we have exchanged contact information. *Pre-CD1*

मार्ग

REFERENCES

Bharati, Dayanand. 2005. *Understanding Hinduism*. New Delhi: Munshiram Manoharlal.

David, George. 1998. *Communicating Christ among Indian Peoples*. Mumbai: GLS.

Frykenberg, Robert Eric. 2008. *Christianity in India: From Beginnings to the Present*. Oxford: Oxford University Press.

Jenkins, Philip. 2008. *The Lost History of Christianity: The Thousand-year Golden Age of the Church in the Middle East, Africa, and Asia—and How It Died*. New York: HarperCollins.

Jones, E. Stanley. 1925. *The Christ of the Indian Road*. New York: Abingdon.

Khan, Benjamin. 1983. *The Concept of Dharma in Valmiki Ramayana*. New Delhi: Munshiram Manoharlal.

Radhakrishnan, S. K. 1927. *The Hindu View of Life*. London: Allen and Unwin.

Webster, John C. B. 2009. *The Dalit Christians: A History*. 3rd ed. Delhi: ISPCK.

CPSIA information can be obtained
at www.ICGtesting.com
Printed in the USA
BVHW060736020720
582581BV00005B/11